YOUTH, WORLD, and CHURCH

YOUTH, WORLD, and CHURCH

WITHDRAWN Sara Little
by Unity Library

JOHN KNOX PRESS
Richmond, Virginia

Library of Congress Catalog Card Number: 68–11684
© M. E. Bratcher 1968
Printed in the United States of America
Item No. 28-1478

Preface

The original invitation to write this book suggested that a "definitive" book on the church's ministry with youth was needed. The invitation was accepted with the request that the word "definitive" be forgotten. Not on any subject would the writer attempt such an assignment. Furthermore, no one could successfully attempt to be definitive in regard to youth ministry in these days. Situations are changing too rapidly, too many factors have to be considered, too many possibilities open up before us. What is offered here, therefore, has a certain tentativeness about it—a deliberate tentativeness. But there is also a conviction behind what is said that this is the right direction for these days, that significant events are springing up in youth ministry, and that some of the ideas presented here or glimpses of happenings may be helpful. Pastors, parents, church officers, teachers, advisers—almost any adult interested in the church's ministry with youth will be interested in what is said.

The youth staff (Ruth D. See, editor; Robert P. Richardson, Jr.; H. William Peterson) of the Board of Christian Education, Presbyterian Church, U.S., has shared at every level in the planning and writing of this book. It is *their* book, too. Young people, adult leaders, pastors and directors of Christian education, denominational board and agency representatives who participated in a series of consultations planned by the youth staff during 1965–66 will recognize their contributions. References to consultations identify some of these comments; at other times, ideas are used without identification.

Several comments are in order by way of explanation and interpretation. Although the approach to youth ministry is considered valid for the six-year span of twelve to eighteen, or seventh through twelfth grades, references and illustrations are made more frequently to older than to younger adolescents. For that reason, *The Young Adolescent in the Church* (Philadelphia: Geneva Press, 1962), a publication of the United Presbyterian Church U.S.A., is recommended as a supporting document, consistent in theory and more directly applicable to the younger group. References are made to this book in several instances.

Accounts of developments are drawn from many denominations and sections of the country, and even beyond the United States. Most frequent references are to the Presbyterian Church, U.S., and to the Covenant Life Curriculum officially in use in six denominations. Such references are illustrative of trends or ideas considered appropriate for use on a wider basis than any one denomination.

Then one word about the "thrust" of the book. Every effort is made to hold in balance the mission and education orientation to youth ministry, and to do this by seeing them as interdependent. But the beginning point is on mission. Often a shift in emphasis is a way of correcting a previous neglect. Often it is a response to a new situation in the world. The long movement of history, or better, the power of the Lord of history, balances and rebalances all our limited efforts to understand and to serve as we build out from the past into a changing present and future. The approach here, then, as we pull out, reflect upon, and build around the idea of the church in mission, is constantly to remind ourselves of the need to keep proper balance and tension with other areas—and to be ready to move on to another emphasis when the time comes for another historical reordering.

One final comment about the book as a whole. The hope is that, as an adult begins to move into the book, he will see possibilities, will want to engage in some new enterprises with new understanding—but that he will not bear a burden of guilt if he cannot reform the church, change the world, and work with youth with unfailing effectiveness in a varied program! (In fact, the writer stands judged by her own words, and hardly dares face again that group of youth in her own congregation.) Further, it is the hope that the actual experience of ministering to and with youth will be rewarding in itself (even though demanding) and that motivation to read further, or to reread, may arise from involvement in doing what the book is talking about.

Books can do only a few things—offer suggestions, glimpses,

stimulate ideas. The faithful work of adults who care is more important than any book on youth ministry can ever be. But if YOUTH, WORLD, AND CHURCH offers any help at all, the writer will be grateful.

SARA LITTLE

Presbyterian School of Christian Education
Richmond, Virginia

Contents

I.
The Ministry of Reconciliation

The Body of Christ lives in the world on behalf of the world, in intercession for the world.

—WILLIAM STRINGFELLOW[1]

The power to discern the presence of the Word of God in common life is the gift of life itself, the restoration of life, the beginning of new life. The power to discern the presence of the Word of God in the world is the knowledge of the Resurrection.

—WILLIAM STRINGFELLOW[2]

1
Thanks Be
to God

The thesis of YOUTH, WORLD, AND CHURCH is this: Youth who are members of the church are called to Christian discipleship *now,* as people of God placed in the world for ministry; they are a part of the ministering Body of Christ, within which they are supported and equipped for the fulfilling of their common calling.

That thesis-sentence is a rather complicated way to begin a book. The adult leader of youth may read with lifted eyebrow the suggestion that the thesis might (just conceivably) begin to answer such familiar questions as these:

Don't you agree that youth work in our church is in a state of emergency?

What is your church doing for Sunday evening programs these days?

How does one get young people to study outside class? Or to be interested in anything *in* class?

What do you think about this idea of doing away with the youth fellowship entirely?

What is it "they" mean when "they" insist that young people and adults should do things together?

Aren't you a little—well, *afraid*—of today's youth?

Who knows what it is we're trying to *do,* anyway?

Some of these questions sound superficial, but they all are indicative of significant issues in what has usually been called "youth work in the church." Collectively, these questions suggest that a kind of *burden* seems to rest on concerned adults. They sound like a comment by an American Baptist leader about the BYF (Baptist Youth Fellowship):

A friend of mine was invited to become an adult advisor to the BYF in his church. He asked me to tell him quite frankly how I would describe the job. My answer was an instantaneous one, absolutely unpremeditated, and I have been haunted by some form of it ever since. I said lightly, "Why, it is like pushing an elephant up a hill."[1]

Not that this book is intended to provide a formula for "pushing an elephant up a hill"! But we do recognize frankly that working with youth is not easy in these days. Ministers, parents, church officers, teachers, advisers—we who have responsibility for youth—often experience something of the distress the Apostle Paul felt in his work with the Corinthians. Yet even in the middle of difficult moments, Paul could break out in expressions of joy and confidence.

But thanks be to God, who in Christ always leads us in triumph, and through us spreads the fragrance of the knowledge of him everywhere.

—2 CORINTHIANS 2:14

Though our situation is different, our motivation, our hope, is the same. Knowing that whatever good is accomplished is by the power of the Holy Spirit, we seek to become channels of that power in the confidence that the church today is commissioned to engage in the ministry of reconciliation—that ministry of which Paul began to write in Second Corinthians shortly after his spontaneous expression of thanksgiving. As we adults contemplate our ministry, we do so as a response of profound gratitude to the God and Father of our Lord Jesus Christ. "Thanks be to God," we say with Paul, as we look toward the difficulties and joys of our work.

What *is* intended in the thesis is to offer a kind of central focus around which we can build an approach to youth work, or as we now more appropriately call it, the church's ministry with youth. The consistent development of this central focus—if this is possible—should give some clues as to how a particular congregation may plan with its youth. It is important that *what* is done should hang together with *why* it is done, so that people (youth as well as adults) who are engaged in the youth ministry enterprise should have understanding and a sense of direction. Needless to say, the ideas offered here will become clear only as they are worked through in particular situations; they are, therefore, only a beginning point.

What is new and distinctive about the approach proposed here? Three phrases from the thesis, selected and interpreted, will point up the most important aspects of the direction in which we seem to be moving.

". . . called to Christian discipleship *now* . . ."

No adult can penetrate the high school community and there become the "scattered church" in the way a young churchman can. The same is true of other circles in the complex youth culture. Their insights and energies enable youth to add a unique contribution as they serve with all ages in the church. Young laity, therefore, are *needed* to engage in Christian mission. The time they spend in church is to be viewed as an opportunity for present ministry, not just as a period of preparation for the real thing later on.

". . . a part of the ministering Body of Christ . . ."

Those who have professed their faith in Jesus Christ and become communicant members are to be viewed as full members. Such a view has much to say about the attitude the congregation takes toward youth, and about the provision it makes for their participation in its worship and work. Even within this fellowship, they give as well as receive, they minister to others as members one of another. Moreover, because the Body of Christ has to do with the church universal, not just a particular congregation, its work must be done in awareness of and relation to what the Apostles' Creed calls "the holy catholic church."

". . . within which they are supported and equipped for . . ."

The thrust toward ministry *now* suggests the direction for the educational task of the church. That task will be oriented toward present calling, not just in an activity-centered program, but in a genuine seeking for ways of being obedient Christian servants in today's world. Members will find meaningful corporate worship within the "communion of saints" an event of major importance.

Almost any experienced worker with youth is probably saying, "That's not new. We've been trying to do that all along." True. Here is no radical discontinuity with the past. The difference is rather a matter of emphasis, a change of focus in why and even how we take hold of and build toward an effective youth ministry. Any such change of focus always brings new dangers. For instance, we face the danger—

of neglecting some important facets of youth ministry. It seems impossible for human beings to see *wholes,* and to keep parts or emphases in proper perspective.

of assuming that the new necessarily is good, the old is bad. Failure to see *why* something was done as it was in the past makes us unable to evaluate and preserve value. We tend to put our trust in newness rather than to respond freely to the ongoing, dynamic activity of God.

of searching for some perfect structure or method to do our job for us without committed effort on our part. No program is ever going to produce results automatically without our own hard work. The search for a perfect external pattern will use up our energies in what has been called "the perennial pursuit of fugitive forms."

And others . . .

Nevertheless, it *is* true that we have made mistakes in the past. Here are some of them.

In the building of a strong nondenominational Christian Endeavor in the late nineteenth and early twentieth centuries, Protestantism developed youth leadership and appreciation of a Christian unity broader than denominational differences; but too often we cultivated a youth church alongside the church. Later, in the building of a strong, closely structured denominational youth fellowship, we helped develop the peer group as a channel of Christian influence and support; but sometimes we built a greater loyalty to a continuing youth organization than to Christ and his church. Our recent tendency to speak of youth of the church, rather than of the youth fellowship (a term first used by the Congregational Christian Churches in 1936), may bring us no nearer to our goal, for neither the latest name nor current terminology in itself will effect desired change. If we do genuinely hold on to the attitudes suggested by the thesis, matters of terminology and organization will take care of themselves, and we will be better able to avoid the mistakes of recent years.

One writer has summarized those mistakes in terms of four heresies:

1. The "future-church" heresy, dealing with young people as the churchmen of tomorrow.

2. The "numbers-game" heresy, measuring success in youth work by the number of young people who can be persuaded to be "active" in one aspect or another of the total youth program.

3. The "street-cleaning" heresy, setting up programs to keep the boys and girls off the street even though secular organizations as well as other churches are also ministering to the same young people.

4. The "stop-gap" heresy, involving young people in a variety of organizations which substitute busy work for solid nurture in the faith and preparation for mission in the world.[2]

The history of any denomination's ministry with its youth would be instructive. Let the early efforts of the Presbyterian Church, U.S., serve to illustrate. That ministry had a modest beginning when Miss Katharine Hawes of Second Presbyterian Church, Richmond, Virginia, first met her Sunday school class of boys for games, reading, and music before her "great log fire" in October, 1895. She started her work with boys because they were not especially interested in the church, she said, and "we felt they needed the work, and that the Church needed them."[3] This was a simple statement of purpose for the first organized youth work in the Presbyterian Church, U.S., but clear enough to guide the "Covenanters" (for so they named themselves) into a movement that spread rapidly throughout the denomination.

Every new effort has made its contributions and its mistakes.

Every effort has involved new and sometimes unexpected problems. In the first decade of this twentieth century, the Superintendent of Sabbath Schools and Young People's Work, Dr. Alexander Lacy Phillips, had to deal with the problem of youth meetings that failed to abide by the General Assembly's stated policy: "Sessions should take care that the women and girls do not transgress the limitations of Scripture by conducting meetings or by engaging in public prayer or exhortation."[4] Though he may have succeeded momentarily, that policy has long been a dead issue.

In the third decade youth work was almost disrupted by controversy stemming from the "frightful error" made in centering a denominational youth conference on the radical discussion method, which called forth "crude and half-baked views from a group of young people who seemed to delight in hearing themselves talk."[5] We smile at the statement today—then we suddenly become aware that we can understand principles only in the context of cultural influences or particular historical incidents.

These changing emphases bring a sense of impermanence or transiency about whatever is undertaken. But the tentative attitude that results is a good thing. The recognition of such changes helps us keep a sense of humor, a touch of lightness, about any specific suggestions which emerge in the development of the thesis stated at the beginning of this chapter.

As we prepare to explore implications of that thesis, we may be helped by three summarizing statements.

First, the direction being suggested here—not a finished program—seems faithful to the gospel and appropriate to the demands of this particular moment in history. But the real test will come when a group of churchmen work out the specifics of their own youth ministry.

Second, the direction seems consistent with that of Protestantism generally. This direction is embodied in the objective of Christian education for senior high youth, which is, indeed, the objective for the Christian education of all ages.

The objective for Christian education is that all persons be aware of God through his self-disclosure, especially his redeeming love as revealed in Jesus Christ, and that they respond in faith and love—to the end that they may know who they are and what their human situation means, grow as sons of God rooted in the Christian community, live in the Spirit of God in every relationship, fulfill their common discipleship in the world, and abide in the Christian hope.[6]

In the terms of this objective, the emphasis in the thesis is on the "common discipleship in the world." In any event, the test for the objective comes when groups work through it until it is understood, and has been either adapted or accepted by a church for its own use in planning and evaluating.

Third, the direction implies that youth ministry today is inextricably bound up with the renewal of the church as a whole. "Thanks be to God," we say, with reverence and fear, as we catch a glimpse of what it means to participate in the ministry of reconciliation. Can that response be characteristic of the life of the whole church?

What, then, is YOUTH, WORLD, AND CHURCH all about? It is a book about the church's ministry to, in behalf of, with, and by, youth. It is about the rationale underlying such a ministry, about possible forms and processes it may take, and about the role of the adult leader.

2

God So Loved
the *World*...

If we take seriously the view that young churchmen are indeed a part of the Body of Christ, then it follows logically that the direction of youth ministry will depend to a large extent on what is influencing the church or going on in the church generally. The position stated in the preceding chapter reflects such dependence. It can be understood better after further exploration of what might be called the church's painful but joyful rediscovery of the world and of the church's mission to the world. Reflection on the two quotations by William Stringfellow at the beginning of this section will point us not only to a call to obedience, but also to the possibility of renewal that may result in the life of the church and of the individual Christian.

It would be difficult to say what the cause is for this rediscovery of the world and of the church's mission. One cause may be the so-called rediscovery of the biblical message earlier this century. Perhaps another is a response to the urgency of problems all around that almost seem to overwhelm us. We stand in both admiration and fear before the rapid expansion of knowledge, the power of man, the forces and life patterns that are emerging in a pluralistic and secularized society. But even as we hesitate, we know it is into *this* world, *now,* that the church must move in mission. Young people are involved in this mission. They are involved in the church's effort to discern and respond to God's actions in the world. Although emphasis on the world and the church's mission in the world of course is not the only determinative influence shaping youth ministry, the nature of that ministry becomes clearer when it is explored in three dimensions of the life of the church: world, mission, and ecumenism.

World

The world was created by God; it is the object of his love, and the scene of his continuing activity. In this sense, *world* refers to the created universe, including man. Like its predecessor, the Jewish community, the church has often considered itself as the sole recipient of God's love and the sole locus of his activity. But again and again the biblical tradition has reasserted itself, and the church has been confronted anew with the Lord of history who works through worldly events to achieve his purpose for all mankind. Nothing is beyond the scope of his concern or his power. His name is Emmanuel, God-with-us.

In many ways, such views simply remind us of the historical nature of Christianity. The new element is more an *affirmation* of the world and an inclination to celebrate, to express joy in, God's presence and activity in the world, even in those places and by those persons not known to be associated with the church. Expressions of this mood are found throughout contemporary Christian writing, both Catholic and Protestant. For example, documents of the recent Second Vatican Council consider church and world as mutually related; they speak of the church's enrichment by the world as well as its service to the world, of dialogue in genuine openness and respect between church and world, of the solidarity of the human race.

These considerations raise many questions in relation to the experiences of youth. How can we help youth understand the biblical view of our Sovereign God so that they may see him choosing to work through scientific developments and political powers? Would youth (and adults as well) find life more meaningful if they viewed *all* life as within his lordship? How can we help youth perceive the presence of his Spirit? Can they learn to reflect theologically on the meaning of events in this constantly changing world, and thereby participate more fully in God's manifestation of his love for the world? How can we help release those aesthetic interests and abilities so characteristic of youth, enabling them to express through varied forms the meaning they perceive?

But there is another side to this picture, the side to which Paul pointed when he warned, "Do not be conformed to this world"

(Rom. 12:2). *World* in this sense means "that spirit of vanity and malice which transforms into an instrument of sin those human energies intended for the service of God and man."[1] That very spirit continues to be a part of man, even the Christian man, and of the church as an institution which is human as well as divine. It unleashes powers of darkness against which man has always had to struggle, powers which seem stronger, more pervasive, than ever before. True, these powers have been conquered in Jesus Christ; but man has not fully appropriated that victory, nor learned that the presence and power of the Holy Spirit can enable him to appropriate it day by day. Instead, man has been enslaved by structures and powers which were meant to be his servants, and he seems unable to break loose.

What can the church do to enable youth to recognize the powers of darkness—the temptation to cheat and steal because of pressure to excel, the drive to conform to "worldly" values set forth by mass media and idolized by his peers, the obsession with sex? In the struggle for youth to become mature in Christ, Christian freedom is set over against enslavement to the world. *It is only as man overcomes his enslavement to the world that he becomes free to enjoy the world.* A part of the rediscovery of the world, then, is a serious call to view realistically the tensions which grip youth (and all men) in this second half of the twentieth century.

Mission

To say that the world is the object of God's love is to point not only to the world but also to God's mission in the world, the mission into which he has called his church.

Mission, as used here, refers to God's action in Jesus Christ by which he is reconciling the world to himself. On the human level, mission refers to the witness of the church to the message of reconciliation, expressed corporately and individually, in word and deed. That witness becomes an instrument for the healing of mankind by the continuing presence of God in his Holy Spirit. Mission is always God's action. But the church shares in what he is doing because Jesus Christ is head of the church. No one action or thing is ever *mission,* because mission refers to the whole of God's activity. Man's specific words or actions can only be evidences of his participation in the great ongoing biblical drama of redemption, or his engagement in the ministry of reconciliation.

Two recent statements will set forth the church's understanding of its role in mission. The first is taken from an official denominational document, the second from a joint declaration of a group of denominations.

> Christ has established his Church in the world that he might have a people to serve him, and that they should be the instruments of his reconciling ministry in the world.
>
> The Christian is sent by his Lord into this world, as the Father sent the Son into this world. He is to live in this world as his Lord lived in the world; love it because God loves it; serve it because his Lord came to serve it and to redeem it.
>
> The primary witness of the Church to her King and Head is made as Christians, obedient to their Lord's commands, love and serve their neighbors for Christ's sake.
>
> The Church witnesses by word and action to the lordship of Christ over human society and to the love, justice and righteousness of God over against the evils of the world; praying ". . . Thy kingdom come. Thy will be done in earth, as it is in heaven."[2]

The second example is found in the statement made by the Consultation on Church Union, in which representatives of eight denominations—increased to ten by March, 1967—declared their conviction that "obedience to mission must be the primary characteristic of the church at every level."[3] The "obedience" of which the Consultation speaks is an expression of faith, a confession in mission that parallels the confession in worship.

> Inheriting the apostolic vocation the united church is called to exercise its reconciling mission, both to individuals and to the power-structures of the world. Its efforts to fulfill this commission will therefore form a major mode of confessing its faith. It will seek continually to clarify its understanding of the eternal gospel, and to convey that understanding in its public appeal to the

world. It will seek to translate the essentials of Christian faith into terms intelligible to men, without weakening the demands which are intrinsic to Christ's work as Judge and Redeemer of all. It will seek to speak to the contemporary issues of public life, knowing the conflict between "the wisdom of God" and "the wisdom of this age," and knowing also that Christ has reconciled the world to God. Serving in Christ's name and example, the Church will translate its faith as it gives itself in suffering love for the world. Only in such translation of faith into deeds will the Church participate in the suffering and glory of the Crucified and Risen Lord. In each situation it will give its grateful witness to the presence of God, who rules and over-rules the affairs of men and nations.[4]

The church is called to work out day by day the implications of declared positions such as these. Only so can it come to understand what such statements actually mean. But are these declarations relevant in a book about youth ministry? Is the mission focus appropriate for youth? The answer is *yes,* for two reasons—both because youth can grow in Christian maturity only as they know in experience the meaning of obedience, and because the church needs youth to be the Christian witness among their contemporaries.

A youth leader relates the role of high school youth in the church directly to mission:

It is this kind of rediscovery of mission which has brought about another revolution in the church's understanding of the role of the young person in its life. So long as the church believed that its primary task was to maintain its own institutional life in order to provide nurture for those within it, youth were necessarily assigned a subordinate role, since they obviously lack the experience and judgment to manage the business affairs of this mammoth institution. But when the church's primary concern shifts from institutional maintenance to mission in the world, then the young person takes his place alongside the adult as another soldier on the firing line. . . . He lives in places which the adult can enter only as a stranger. He has relationships with

other young persons who are, in many cases, removed from relationship with adults by a wall of suspicion and prejudices.[5]

One might not agree with some of the views implied—for example, the judgment that the church has consciously neglected mission
for institutional maintenance; but it would be hard to disagree with
the argument that youth are strategically placed for mission.

Moreover, in their dislike of sham, their readiness for action,
their hint of idealism, their restless energy, youth seem to suggest
that *mission* almost more than any other is the idea which might
speak to them relevantly about the nature of the Christian faith.
Youth's response to the Peace Corps, or the testimony of some that
the church and faith became real to them for the first time in a sit-in
or a march to protest racial injustice, should remind us of certain inadequacies in our traditional work with youth.

Several years ago a delightful redheaded teen-ager named
Sue—serious, full of vitality—made an impassioned plea to the
adult leader at a youth conference after a discussion on the church
and poverty. "Here we are ready to do something, *dying* to do
something, and stop all this talking which just leaves us feeling
guilty and frustrated," she said. "Why is it you adults do us this
way? You get us steamed up, and then, when we feel we *must* do
something, you have nothing to suggest, no concrete ways for us to
take hold. Or you slow us down on our own ideas with cautions and
warnings. What is the church anyway?" Many things are pointed up
in Sue's comments: youth's desire for action; its impatience with in-
consistency of word and deed; the need for competent and committed adults who understand the dangers in Christian education which
provides motivation with no clear vision of channels for response.
All these are involved in an understanding of mission as a focus for
work with youth.

But *mission* cannot, must not, be interpreted as a new gimmick
to put vitality into youth work. Whatever relevance it has to youth
comes from its reality as a power in a whole church consumed with
a desire to be obedient. Effective ministry to youth is dependent
upon renewal of the church, a renewal which is evidenced here and
there. If the concept—and the actuality—of mission to the world

can continue to be a force for renewal of the church, young people as members will benefit through their participation in the ongoing life of the Body of which Jesus Christ is the head. Youth's impatience and energy may become a gift to the church which the younger generation offers as a prod to mission and to renewal.

Mission, then, is the church's reason for existence. The church exists not for itself, but for others—for the world of which it is a part and to which it is a distinct, contrasting entity. It exists to witness to Jesus Christ in both word and deed as it enters into his reconciling ministry to individuals and to society. Its maintenance of its own life through worship, nurture, fellowship, education, is an integral part of its mission—for how else would it be sure that its witness would be to the God and Father of our Lord Jesus Christ rather than to some fleeting idol? But this maintenance of its life is also a preparation for its mission expressed in outgoing concern, in servanthood, in love willing to suffer. This latter emphasis is predominant here when the term *mission* is used, but never in exclusion from other functions of the church. The degree to which mission brings together, unites, incarnates, all these dimensions of the life of the church is an indication of whether the church is engaged in Christian mission or in empty activity easily equated with works-righteousness.

Ecumenism

Ecumenism has to do with the effort to make visible the unity which already belongs to the church as God's gift to it. Two recent emphases lead to certain implications for the church's ministry with youth—the relationship of ecumenism to renewal and reform, and its relationship to mission.

Consider the first emphasis. The ecumenical movement makes us think of those activities and organizations which foster unity among Christians, and promote mutual respect and understanding of doctrine and practice among various communions. Ecumenism, however, does not stop at trying to understand distinctive features and contributions; it moves beneath the surface to underlying unity, and to the church's examination of its own faithfulness. This examination leads to concern for renewal and reform, which are related to ecumenism, as they are to mission. Indeed, in the words of the Second Vatican Council, there is no ecumenism "worthy of the name" without church renewal and "change of heart." "Christ summons the Church, as she goes her pilgrim way, to that continual reformation of which she always has need, insofar as she is an institution of men here on earth."[6]

This view of a pilgrim church and a pilgrim people should strike a responsive note in Protestantism, with its traditional view that the church must always be in the process of being reformed.

The second emphasis, concern for mission, is also linked with the ecumenical dimension of the life of the church. When Christians are drawn together in a genuine seeking to minister to and in the world, barriers of age and race and class disappear. So do denominational barriers.

Focus on mission, or on the world and its needs, according to Albert van den Heuvel, who was in the Youth Department of the World Council of Churches, may well be the proper area of concentration for the ecumenical movement in these times. He calls for a "secular understanding of the ecumenical," which he says recaptures something of the original meaning of ecumenical as referring to the whole inhabited earth. "The basic element of this understanding is that the ecumenical movement does not speak so much about the relations among the churches, but relations between the church and the world."[7]

Many scholars who would disagree with this use of the term "ecumenical" would find it harder to disagree with the practical conclusions drawn from Van den Heuvel's belief that churches might find in service the unity and integrity they fail to find in intellectualizing. Indeed, we cannot first clarify relations among the churches before we seek to minister. Involvement in mission is a surer road to ecumenicity than is "comparative ecclesiology."

> ... the only way to a renewed church is the common witness and service to the good news in the world. What is the use ... of a united church which is not united in a real struggle for faithfulness in society? What does it help us to be united on doctrine and order if to the world we only look like a bigger and better ghetto?

What is the use of a united liturgy if it does not spring fresh from a direct and common dialogue within the world in which we worship publicly? What is the use of a doctrinal consensus the theologians have sweated out if this common kerygma is not understood in the society where it is formulated? Or what is the use of an answer—which we proudly work out together—to a question which nobody in the world is asking? What is the use of a ministry accepted and recognized by all Christians if the ministers are not indeed engaged in the Messianic ministry to the world?[8]

What does all this say about the church's ministry with youth? First of all, it is another challenge to the church to be the church. Again drawing on Albert van den Heuvel, we note his view that ". . . the real goal of the ecumenical movement is an authentic Christian community in each place."[9] Young people need to be full participants in that kind of community. They need to share in the congregation's search for structures through which it may engage more effectively in mission in these times. That search will call for elimination of competition or duplication of effort, and for a united witness to the lordship of Christ.

In the second place, it calls for recognition of the fact that young people are in what might be called an "ecumenical situation" in the high school. What can be done to help young people be truly representative of the whole church as they transcend denominational barriers in this ministry which is peculiarly their own? They must not be isolated from the church, but prepared and supported by it if they are to *be* that church. Their faith, even their awareness of the distinctiveness of their own confessional heritage, may be clarified and strengthened as they engage in dialogue with others, both Christian and non-Christian. As they unite in service, they can know more fully the meaning of giving vitality to the one church, for "the participants in the ecumenical movement are *all those who care* and who are willing to test their faith in effective expressions of it."[10]

Some such dimensions of the life of the church as the three suggested in this chapter seem especially significant for the church's work with youth in the latter part of the twentieth century. The big question coming to us from every angle is this: Will the church allow itself to be reformed and renewed, in order that it may express God's love for his world?

3
God's Own People

What is the basis for the view that the church's youth ministry is so to be shaped that Christian youth will be included as responsible participants in the church's mission to the world? Quite simply, such a view rests on the conviction that terms like "a royal priesthood, a holy nation, God's own people" (1 Peter 2:9) refer to *all* those who profess faith in Jesus Christ. They share in the ministry which is committed to the church. Such a statement must be explored further, not only in terms of what it means, but also in terms of what it does not mean.

Young Laity

References to "ministry" as a task given to the whole church may have been misleading to some readers. This interpretation is consistent with a recovery of the Reformation—and biblical—view of the priesthood of the Body of Christ. The fact is that the word "ministry" is "*not* used in the Bible to designate a special group within the Church,"[1] thus separating clergy and laity. Rather, the clergy is ordained to a particular role of service to and with the church, a service of equipping other members for the carrying out of their task. But all believers and their children "are *baptized* into the Christian priesthood. And everyone who is baptized shares fully, and should share equally, in their priesthood of the body."[2] *Young laity*, then, are called to contribute their particular gifts, to assume their specific tasks within the overall division of function and labor. They receive and respond to the gospel, and are equipped for their service, as *laity,* as *parts* of the church, not as a separate organization.

Questions about practical implications of such generalized theological statements arise at once and need to be examined.

1. Does the attention to "young laity" indicate a lack of concern for young people who are outside the church?

No.

It does suggest involving young laity in planning for ministry to outsiders, either by finding ways to meet them on their own territory, or inviting them into the church fellowship. The goal in this effort is not membership recruitment, although we need not oppose or be indifferent about inviting youth to join, afraid that we will be accused of the "numbers" heresy. If what we find through the church is indeed "good news," then we will want to share it.

Church youth are aware that often they are not *really* viewed as "a part." This was illustrated while the author was working with six or seven young people in the preparation of an eleventh-twelfth grade text, *The Language of the Christian Community*. In the manuscript the young people read this statement: *"This book is addressed to those 'within the faith.'* That is to say, the assumption is that you are a Christian. The perspective is that of 'faith seeking understanding.' "[3] The ensuing conversation ran something like this:

JIM: Do you really mean that?

AUTHOR: Yes. Why?

JIM: Because people don't usually think about us like that. Adults are the Christians, and even if we are members, they are still working on us to get *us* to be Christian.

MARY: Yes, somebody's always doing something *to* us.

JIM: I like that business about "within the faith." Not that we're *good*—"

MARY: Adults who are Christians aren't always good, either.

JIM: No. But all of us who call ourselves Christian have kind of taken a stand. We have something to start from. And I like to feel that I'm being taken seriously.

The conversation moved to deeper levels—the meaning of the Christian faith as distinguished from but related to goodness; the danger in judging either the goodness or the quality of faith in others; the meaning of commitment. It ended with a consideration of their own responsibility for those who had not "taken a stand," including among other things the possibility of inviting their participation in varied activities of the church in order that they might come "to see and experience the meaning of this faith from the inside."[4] This view of themselves as young laity enabled these young people to see better the responsibilities related to their expressed commitment. In the process they became aware of the possibility of strengthening the church's ministry to the outsider.

2. Does emphasis on participation in the whole life of the church mean that a youth organization is not recommended?

Yes and no.

We can recognize the need for some structure, some organizational plan, to relate young people as organically as possible to the worship and work of the congregation, and then to supplement whatever is done congregationally with appropriate youth activities. The organization will not be designed to unify youth as youth so much as to unify and involve youth with the church. When plans are made for youth ministry, the beginning point is what is offered to the congregation; the secondary level is what is needed in addition for youth.

More specific suggestions about organization are given in chapters 9 and 11. The important point to be made here is that *whatever* plan is used, one should be aware of its major thrust, of what it is intended to do, so that it can be an effective instrument.

3. Does viewing them as young laity mean that young people should be placed on all church committees?

No.

What it means more than anything else is that a certain *attitude* should be characteristic of adults in the congregation. That attitude will influence the way adults speak to and about young people; it will express itself in all kinds of varied ideas that will surprise even the sensitive adults who think of big and little ways to include youth; it will be as evident in the way adults help plan youth-only activities as in the adult-youth relationships in congregational activities. Placing youth on church committees may be just an empty external formula used to excuse adults from the attitude of inclusion and respect.

Placing youth on committees *may* help, on the other hand. In this connection it is important to recognize levels of maturity in the six-year span of youth. Differences in interests and abilities of youth within this span necessitate care in deciding what tasks can appropriately be assumed by an individual. Ordinarily, long-range responsibilities can be undertaken better by older teen-agers; more specific, short-term responsibilities, by younger persons. For example, a twelfth grader might serve on a church committee for a year's appointment. A seventh grader might be invited to serve on a task force to get ready for a youth-adult work day at the church or in the community. More specific suggestions for the younger age are to be found in *The Young Adolescent in the Church,* cited in the Preface.

Ways to express the attitude of inclusion will occur to adults. Among the possibilities are short-term youth-adult study groups, parent-youth panels or seminars, service groups. It is important to help youth understand worship so they can enter into it more meaningfully. Finally, however, each congregation must find its own ways to include youth.

Youth and Their Situation

Young laity are also young people, conditioned by their culture. This fact should influence policy, strategy, program, in the approach to youth.

To be realistic, we must admit that some of the terms we have used in identifying young Christians with the people of God seem far removed from the teen-agers whom we know and with whom we work. In an interview in preparation for the writing of this book, young people were requested to give advice to adult leaders. "Have a thick skin, or you'll never survive working with us," one young person said. Others agreed. After general assent to the question of whether it would be "a good thing" for youth to serve on church committees, one girl commented, "But you can't always count on us. We're irresponsible." As an afterthought, someone else added, "I guess a lot of the trouble between youth and adults is our fault." Honest self-appraisal, to say the least!

Mr. Douglas Sarff, a tenth and eleventh grade English teacher in Wayzata, Minnesota, was honest, even harsh, in some of the comments he made about high school students. In fact, he paid $140 for a full-page ad in the local weekly, *The Minnetonka Herald,* to say what he thought about the youth and the community that produced them.

> . . . to get a general picture of what makes me splenitive, step into a classroomful of this year's seniors and take a look. Wear an overcoat against the chill, though—because, Dear Reader, they are frozen solid with sophistication. Any value dearly held, whether by teacher or fellow-student, and any emotion produced by any value, are killed by sneering indifference. No matter what the value, no matter what the motion, a cold draft fills the atmosphere.[5]

This "mass of bored, indifferent, dulled mediocrities or tittering good timers," Sarff said, "are dead in every sense of the word except viscerally." Because he had seen enough of "living death," he felt compelled to criticize the "slick, empty, 'modern living' " from which youth assimilated its values. The school, he said, was a reflection of the community, more concerned with "good public relations" than with "the teaching of wisdom." Or again:

> There is too much "how-to-be-popular" propagandizing, with a meaningless smile and a slapped back substituting for genuine affection, so that the young learn how (in Wordsworth's phrase) to extend "greetings where no kindness is." As for the churches, they have become mere social centers for mother-daughter and father-son banquets and the like. Able to teach only a diluted religion, they function chiefly as exemplars of the hypocrisy of the times.[6]

Mr. Sarff resigned his teaching position, because he could not "bear to witness gentleness turned sour and curiosity turned to sophistication," and because he saw the community and its school, which produced such results, as "a diseased organism."

Whether Mr. Sarff's accusations were or were not justified is beside the point. He obviously *cared* about young people, and saw the truth that the world is the matrix from which values are derived.

Socrates, too, spoke disparagingly of youth in the fifth century
B.C. A remark attributed to him declares:

> Youth today loves luxury. They have bad manners, have con-
> tempt for authority, no respect for older people, and talk non-
> sense when they should work. Young people do not stand up any
> longer when adults enter the room. They contradict their parents,
> talk too much in company, guzzle their food, lay their legs on the
> table and tyrannize their elders.[7]

The remark is not quoted to show that young people are always
the same—and therefore hopeless! Rather, it is meant to indicate
that whatever is problematic about adolescents must be viewed
against the background of the culture of a given time and nation. As
interpreted by Albert H. van den Heuvel, Socrates' famous comment referred to youth whose disobedience and bad manners were
marks of the decay of Greek culture, when adults "no longer produced the clear leadership and inspiration that could be accepted
happily by the young adults."[8]

It seems that in each culture, before it declines or before exis-
tential changes take place in it, such a strain is put on the younger
generation that they feel compelled to rebel and show in their
conduct their unrest and uncertainty about the future. Whenever
this happens, they are described as revolutionaries or nihilists by
the adults (whose reactions always seem to be the same). *Adolescence as distinct human behavior emerges when a society is no
longer stable.* The normal physical changes that occur in the early
teens are accompanied by spiritual changes, which prolong the
period of unrest and instability until their own participation in the
changing society is allowed or made possible.[9]

Whether adults rise up to say in protest that society is not so sick
as it is often portrayed, or to admit in repentance that society is far
from achieving God's purposes for it, the fact remains that young
people are a part of a culture with contradictory values and nebulous goals.

In today's world, any mention of the impact of culture on youth must take into account the changes effected by the electronic age, with its computers, its television, its other media. Marshall McLuhan, popular and controversial Canadian professor and writer, contends that our whole environment is changing through the technology we have developed as extensions of ourselves, and that we are changing in the way we see, feel, perceive. *We are being changed ourselves into different kinds of creatures.* He makes a strong case for his view. For example, it was the advent of the written word which, by Plato's time, made possible the detribalization of man. With the passing of the mechanical age and the advent of the electric age, "our central nervous system is technologically extended to involve us in the whole of mankind and to incorporate the whole of mankind in us ..."[10]

One clear effect seems to be that youth can no longer be isolated from the adult world. The compression of the world has become an "implosive factor that alters the position of the Negro, the teen-ager, and some other groups. They can no longer be *contained,* in the political sense of limited association."[11] They are immediately involved in our lives, and we in theirs, through mass media.

Another effect that seems clear to McLuhan is that public education is already changing rapidly, and awaits even more radical change.

> In education the conventional division of the curriculum into subjects is already as outdated as the medieval trivium and quadrivium after the Renaissance. Any subject taken in depth at once relates to other subjects. Arithmetic in grade three or nine, when taught in terms of number theory, symbolic logic, and cultural history, ceases to be mere practice in problems. Continued in their present patterns of fragmented unrelation, our school curricula will insure a citizenry unable to understand the cybernated world in which they live.[12]

A report to the federal government calls attention to trends and developments for the next two decades, including those in the field of education, which agencies concerned with youth should antici-

pate. Donald N. Michael, the author of the report, is a social psy-
chologist with a varied background in research and work with
governmental and scientific agencies. His investigation and consultation led him to the conclusion that "profound changes in the procedures, substance, and spirit of the educative processes" are required.[13] His conclusion applies to education throughout life, not
just to school. As programmed instruction, nongraded schools, and
other structures and methods make more effective education possible, pressures will increase, especially on the elite students, and they
will find themselves "more anxious, more competitive, more
'hemmed-in' earlier in their education."[14] The feeling of isolation
and inferiority of unskilled and underprivileged students will increase, according to Michael, and the relation of education to a
complex society will become increasingly problematic.

Youth, then, as well as adults, are faced with the tension of trying to live responsibly and freely. Church youth as well as nonchurch youth are subjected to tremendous pressures (the powers of
darkness mentioned in the preceding chapter), and are the object of
exploitation by those who have made them into a profitable teen-age
consumer's market. This is the situation in which they live. It is not
an easy one. But it is the one in which Christian youth are to find,
be prepared for, and fulfill, their role as young laity.

The future does not seem easier—although in the unexplored
there is always possibility, hope, challenge. In the report by Donald
Michael, the prediction is made that new developments will only in-
tensify the conflict in values and the need for unifying meaning in
an increasingly complex society. Churchmen will be discouraged by
his prediction about the impact of religion:

> But the power and influence of the major religious denominations
> in the next two decades will not be substantially greater or less
> than today. Local religious leaders will seldom be able to bring
> the issues of the spirit to bear on the daily actions of private citi-
> zens and public figures. For just as today, it will be too distracting
> in the marketplace to reconcile God with a rationalizing society.[15]

The church concerned with youth cannot escape its own need

for renewal, *nor its responsibility for society*. It is important for adult leaders to be able to plan a program or lead a discussion group at church, but it is not enough.

Moreover, adolescents themselves may increasingly assume responsibility for shaping culture, rather than being shaped by it. Thereby *their* contribution is made to adult society and to history. As René Maheu, Director-General of Unesco, has said, "Our purpose . . . must be to help the younger generations to be themselves so that youth's eternal promise of regenerating the world is never lost."[16]

Youth as Adolescents

Young laity are also adolescents, a kind of subculture when viewed collectively, a kind of stage of seeking identity in the life cycle when viewed individually. They are affected by their own adolescent stage of development—a fact to be taken into account when considering what youth need from the church and what they are able to offer in ministry.

Adolescent Subculture

More than half the world's population today is under the age of twenty-five—over 1,000 million.[17] This is not a minority group. It is hard to tell whether the influence from general culture toward youth is greater or less than that from youth toward the adult world. Grace and Fred Hechinger are of the opinion, for instance, that the youth market (pre-teen, subteen, teen-age) has been a "stepping-stone for total take-over by youth of the entire United States market."[18] (Reflection on images, standards, values, might lead one to the troubling conclusion that adults have taken over many of the less worthy values of youth, and failed to incorporate those which are more worthy.) The following report says a great deal about the adult world as well as about adolescents.

The orthodox, conservative teen-age market, anno 1965, is still described by cultural historians and market researchers as something definable. The current estimate is $13,000,000,000 a year in freely disposable cash—cash not required for the teen-agers' own maintenance, such as room, board, basic clothing, transportation and schooling. Viewed in this old-fashioned way, the market has expanded by about $3,000,000,000 annually within the past two years and is expected to be well above $20,000,000,000 by 1970. And those statisticians who count the youth market—the age range of thirteen to twenty-two rather than fifteen to nineteen—say that it has already reached about $25,000,000,000.[19]

What happened, according to the Hechingers, is that the teen-age market was "the product of a new concept of the ages of man."

That vague no-man's-land of adolescence, which used to stand between child and adulthood like an unavoidable gap to be bridged and crossed (as quickly as possible, with a stiff upper lip and a prayer), was suddenly turned into a way of life. It became a subculture rather than a transition.[20]

To speak of adolescent subculture as a "way of life" is not quite the same thing as to refer to an age group. We must develop strategy for youth ministry in light of the culture. The point has been made repeatedly that only young laity, who can understand that way of life from within and so penetrate it, are in strategic positions for outreach. Here it should be said that all Christian adults would benefit from an understanding of the adolescent culture of their particular communities.

In one church, for example, a couples' club searching for a program casually mentioned some joint activity with senior highs. The result of this casual remark was a significant evening in which all ages, from junior highs to the oldest member of the church, got better acquainted through the songs and dances most popular with that particular group of youth.

The sounds and movements that appeal to youth interpret their culture. For one night, adults had the privilege of participating in that youth world, through hearing it interpreted and offering their own interpretations. Young people chose the songs and classified the lyrics in various categories. The audience listened to songs in each category; discussion centered around panels of three youth and three adults.

> Among all the songs discussed, the liveliest and most varied opinion was elicited in the category entitled "Songs of Social Protest" by Barry McGuire's "Eve of Destruction," a pounding folk-rock number which wails:
> Don't you understand what I'm try'n to say?
> Can't you feel the fear I'm feelin' today?
> If the button is pushed there's no running away
> There'll be no one to save with the world in a grave.[21]

The evening was a memorable one, as is always the case when age barriers are crossed in genuine communication. Parents of teen-agers "confessed they had never realized some of the pop songs had serious lyrics."[22] As for the young people—

> In being invited to a joint discussion of matters which have such currency and importance in their thought world, they felt they were being taken seriously. Though there was much solidarity among the youth, they felt free to disagree with each other, as well as to agree with certain adults. One could sense that the young people were deeply involved in the experience, and that they were deeply aware of those adults who were—and those who were *not*—accepting them as real persons.[23]

Young people do not seem to be saying to adults, "Become like us. Join our world." In fact, they reject the phony adult. They *are* saying, "Try to understand our world and respect us as individuals within that world." About respect—but what can we say to one another that would enable us to acquire that basic attitude? We can work at the understanding of a way of life as we try to see what is expressed through music, dance, the arts, the thought forms, clothing, patterns of socializing. This understanding may help us to develop activities and programs more likely to appeal to youth than are those we often use, whose forms are actually foreign to their adolescent culture. Church youth, out of politeness or because of parental authority, may endure a boring filmstrip (after a James Bond movie the night before!), but the response of nonchurch youth is a different matter. And we are concerned about those outside as well as inside the church. Illustrations given later in the book follow through implications of these paragraphs.

Adolescent Development

To speak of the adolescent subculture is one thing. To speak of adolescence as a stage of growth toward adulthood is another. Our difficulty in describing maturity or in knowing what it is to be adult in the contemporary world makes it hard to describe adolescence either as contrast to or preparation for adulthood. As a matter of fact, it is misleading to speak of adolescence generally, anyway, when we compare a seventh grader and a twelfth grader. The span of changes between ages twelve and eighteen is illustrated in shifts such as these:

From awkwardness and self-consciousness about changes in the body, to a degree of poise and self-acceptance in the full development of physical and intellectual capacities.

From great outbursts of energy and activity alternating with fatigue and withdrawal, to greater ability in sustained use of energies and loyalties.

From intellectual curiosity and active pursuit of facts and their relationships, to concern with ethical issues and probing for the meaning of ideas.

From dependence on the family, to loyalty to the gang or group, to the beginning development of intimate friendships.

From involvement in present activities, to involvement in the future, in terms of life goals and life companions.

Physical, biological changes accompanying puberty explain some of the turmoil and unpredictability of youth. Sociological forces operative as their allegiance moves from the family to the peer group explain some of the family tensions that develop. Psychological needs to develop a self-image, which beset a person who is both child and adult, or now one, now the other, help us understand the quick changes in attitudes and behavior that baffle us.

In the final analysis, however, awareness of the nature of change in the youth span, or even generalized understanding of the reasons for that change, is less helpful than coming to know the particular young people with whom we adults are most closely associated. We must hear what they say, to know how they feel, in order to appreciate what their fears and values and determining images are. We may find that many of our assumptions are incorrect. This was true with many adults in one research project, when over 2,500 adults, both pastors and laymen, gave their interpretation of youth concerns in a comprehensive study of 2,952 high school Lutheran youth. According to Merton Strommen, the director of the study, the assumption had been that "adults have a fairly accurate picture of this age group," an assumption which is not supported by the data of the study.

> Adults do not have an accurate perception of their congregation's youth. On the contrary they often hold a stereotyped image of youth that dulls their sensitivity to youth's uniqueness and individuality. This image, distorted and unrealistic, tends to encourage an approach to youth that is often irrelevant. How this image was formed is not known. But certainly the mass media have helped to strengthen what now exists.[24]

Through the research, Merton Strommen was able scientifically to categorize many of the problems and characteristics of the Lutheran young people and to help correct the distorted image. He concluded, however, that although reports of averages were valuable in providing a conceptual framework for understanding church youth, "it is the individual in his uniqueness who must be known."[25]

Even isolated comments from individual youth can help us become aware of the uniqueness. Consider several such comments; reflect on what they "say."

Many people the world over have come to know Anne Frank, the thirteen-year-old Jewish girl who wrote a diary when she was hiding from the Nazis, in Holland, with her family. Her entry for February 12, 1944, was this:

The sun is shining, the sky is a deep blue, there is a lovely breeze and I'm longing—so longing—for everything. To talk, for freedom, for friends, to be alone. And I do so long . . . to cry! I feel as if I'm going to burst, and I know that it would get better with crying; but I can't, I'm restless, I go from one room to the other, breathe through the crack of a closed window, feel my heart beating, as if it is saying, "Can't you satisfy my longings at last?"

I believe that it's spring within me, I feel that spring is awakening, I feel it in my whole body and soul. It is an effort to behave normally, I feel utterly confused, don't know what to read, what to write, what to do, I only know that I am longing . . . ![26]

Chris Wienk, a seventeen-year-old interviewed by *Esquire* reporters, comments on adults:

Adults are their own worst enemy. I mean, my dad's trying to learn the twist and all. They try too hard and they do it all the wrong way. They'll read a book on teen psychology, and that's no good. There's no real talk between kids and adults. I mean, whoever talks to their parents about sex anymore?[27]

Ruth, a Lutheran youth fellowship officer, wrote an essay for the youth research mentioned earlier. In it, she said this:

One thing that I would never want my pastor or parents to know is the way my boyfriend and I make love. I wish younger kids would not go steady so soon and for so long.[28]

A group of "shop boys" in vocational training, interviewed by David Mallery, conveyed to him their feeling of inferiority and isolation as they compared themselves with college preparatory students. Thus one could say, "Around here you're *nothing* if you're not college prep."[29] Another, in commenting on something that seemed really valuable to him about school, said, "I had an English teacher last year, and he made you feel like a man as soon as you entered the room."[30]

Such quotations could go on endlessly. All would introduce us to the inner world of the adolescent. In general, however, perhaps it might be said that at least four recurring themes run through expressions of the teen years, usually unverbalized and unconscious hopes or needs, expressing themselves in varied forms, to greater or lesser degrees of clarity and intensity.

I want to be ME

The struggle for identity is what many people see as the central task of adolescence—to establish oneself as a unique, existing individual. It is a plea for independence, for recognition and response. The achievement of identity is one essential step in the human life cycle on which Erik Erikson, psychiatrist and Harvard professor, focuses attention in the system he has developed through his clinical work and his study of life histories.[31] Most people have come to recognize the importance of acquiring basic trust in oneself and one's environment during infancy as the foundation of a healthy personality. But other stages of life are important too, according to Erikson. Failure to pass successfully through the crisis of each stage may make it difficult to move to the next level of development. In order to see the adolescent in perspective, Erikson's scheme is outlined here, giving a central task for each stage:

Infancy: Trust
Early Childhood: Autonomy
Play Age: Initiative
School Age: Industry
Adolescence: Identity
Young Adulthood: Intimacy
Adulthood: Generativity (mature adult's interest in contributing
    to his own and the next generation)
Senescence: Integrity

In such a scheme there is danger in assuming that each stage has a characteristic trait, a simple virtue, that can and should be acquired as a permanent possession. Actually, the same hazards must be faced and reconquered again and again. A task may be prolonged indefinitely, as Erikson says happened with Martin Luther, whose search for identity extended into adulthood, and in fact became fused with the crises related to intimacy and generativity.[32] In Martin Luther, however, we can see dramatically how the acquiring of an ideology, a set of values, an ability to discipline work patterns toward the fulfillment of a vocation, contributed toward the establishment of identity. Elements of the same struggle face maturing youth today, a struggle which can be better understood in the context of the life cycle.

A youth's search for identity is a matter of self-definition, of trying to establish clearly for himself and others who he is. Erikson says, however, that the young person does not go around asking, "Who am I?"

> Nor does the person with a secure sense of identity usually stop to think or to brag about the fact that he has this priceless possession, and of what it consists. He simply feels and acts predominantly in tune with himself, his capacities, and his opportunities; and he has the inner means and finds the outer ways to recover from experiences which impair this feeling. He knows where he fits (or knowingly prefers not to fit) into present conditions and developments.[33]

In his work with mentally ill youth, Erikson discovered that many were "suffering so seriously from a feeling of being (or, indeed, wanting to be) 'nobody' that they were withdrawing from reality."[34] Here was a kind of identity diffusion. In the case of others, there was sometimes a negative identity, a seemingly deliberate taking-on of negative or delinquent characteristics.

In the kind of electronic age before us, many people predict problems greater than ever before in achieving selfhood. Others believe this is not necessarily the case. In any event, each age has to find, for itself, what it means to say that man is made in the image of God, that he is the child of God. Somewhere in that realm lies help for the Christian young person seeking identity.

I want to make a difference

Perhaps this theme is another variation of the first. In part, the way a person establishes identity is by doing something *he* can do,

by making a significant contribution. The mood is captured by a
poem many high school youth study in their American literature.

> I feel me near to some High Thing
>   That earth awaits from me,
> But cannot find in all my journeying
>   What it may be.
>
> I get no hint from hall or street,
>   From forest, hill, or plain,
> Save now a sudden quickening of my feet,
>   Now some wild pain.
>
> I only feel it should be done,
>   As something great and true,
> And that my hands could build it in the sun,
>   If I but knew.[35]

Perhaps "I want to make a difference" is also a search for meaning. Several years ago, in a lay school of theology for barbers and
beauticians, one of the participants said at the concluding session, "I
came here eager to discuss the question, 'Who am I?' I have some
ideas about that now, and I'm glad. But now I know *why* I am, and
that's more important."

Why am I? In a world where one can no longer always see clearly the difference one's work makes, and where isolated acts seem unrelated to any overarching meaning, the question will get harder to
deal with. Oversimplified and pat answers are worthless. The young
person wants to find what Kierkegaard calls "the truth for *me*."

I want to be a part

To be a part of a group, whether it be an elite clique or a gang,
seems essential for the youth. But there is far more to the matter
than that. One takes on the identity of that to which he feels that he
belongs. Or, approached another way, it is only as one gives himself
to a cause greater than he is that he becomes himself. That whole of
which he is a part gives him purpose, a framework for living; it
draws him out of isolation and littleness and loneliness, into the full-

ness of life, into becoming that which he was called to be.

One's significance rests not just within himself. If there is no awe, no reverence, no consciousness of something greater than oneself, where is the possibility of significance? Of commitment?

Belonging to the church, theoretically, potentially, operates in some such way as to offer the "whole" of which one can be a part, the "cause" within which one finds significance. That is the reason this chapter on the people of God is used as a framework for the consideration of adolescence. "God's own people" *include* young Christians who also are adolescents. They are a part of the Body of Christ, and in that fact lies the possibility for identity and for meaning. The individual is related to the Head, Jesus Christ, as part of his Body.

Consciousness of being a "part" sustains an individual as he becomes a Christian witness in the place where he is in the world, whether he be youth or adult. But in speaking of the witness of young Christians as the scattered church, in high school or elsewhere, we are in danger of forgetting how quickly meaning is lost apart from the gathered church.

I want to love and be loved

In her diary, Anne Frank voiced the need to find one real friend who would understand.[36] This need is a seeking for love. The young person's reaching out, sometimes awkwardly, sometimes tenderly, in sex relationships, is often an effort to touch life at its core, in its deepest level of reality.

But what is love? Surely more than commercialized sensuality. Surely more than any of our definitions of it. Sometimes in the family, sometimes in association with truly free human beings, there is the foreshadowing of the healing, freeing, perfect love of God. And the most important thing that can happen to the young person (or to anyone) is for him to come to respond to the love of God in Christ. It is assumed here that the church is potentially a channel through which God confronts youth with his infinite love, and calls him to response. As Lewis Sherrill says, "the path to the deepest self-discovery and the utmost self-release lies within the two-fold experience of knowing oneself loved with infinite love, and of giving love in return 'with all the heart, soul, mind, and strength.' " He adds, "Thus the deepest that is within the universe is calling to the deepest in youth. It is the role of the church to present this call to youth as fact, as promise, and as claim."[37]

What, then, is to be said about the church's ministry with young laity? Essentially, that it is inseparable from the ministry of reconciliation. Adolescents find their identity through their discipleship among the people of God, and in the process, help renew that people through their questions, their contributions, and their confirmation of the purpose unifying the church. What is said in later chapters about specifics of youth ministry will be understandable primarily in terms of presuppositions which have been interpreted in these first chapters.

II.
Involvement
in Mission

As thou didst send me into the world, so I have sent them into the world.

—JOHN 17:18

4
Illustrative Studies:
Scenes of Ministry

Does the Christian mission always express itself in recognizable forms or acts? Is it possible by observing a service project to label it as a genuine, valid expression of mission? Probably not. The same act could express mission when performed by one group, and hypocrisy or busyness for another, depending on the need, the motive, the manner of doing the task. Imitation of something someone else has done, therefore, is always risky. Promotion of certain kinds of activities by adult leaders or denominational and interdenominational executives (or even writers!) is equally risky.

On the other hand, consideration of some things that have been done—things which just possibly are faithful ministries—could be suggestive, could spark in others alertness to situations and stimulate their imagination. The attitude of awareness which prompts new responses to need in particular situations is to be distinguished from the imitative activities which tend to bypass the demanding process of caring and thinking through what should be done, as well as why it should be done.

The three studies presented in this chapter are intended to be illustrative only. The term "scenes of ministry" was suggested by the title *Scenes of Witness,* a booklet issued by the Reformed Church in America as "a series of accounts from congregations depicting the Church in mission."[1] Those accounts show a variety of ways in which the people of God (including youth) are endeavoring to live out their covenant responsibility. Accounts selected for analysis here deal with youth in three different kinds of situations. Reflections on these suggestive acts or activities may be helpful in coming to understand more clearly what is meant by involvement in mission.

A Christian Speaks in a High School Situation

In the fall of 1958, the problem of racial integration in the high schools was intense. A certain school board, taking account of a forty-five-man strike to prevent the attendance of thirteen Negro students, was holding a public hearing for an anti-integration White Citizens' Council. All present were astonished when there stood up a fifteen-year-old grocer's daughter named Jessie Angeline Evans, a straight-A junior in the high school and president of the student council. Angie reported on a test poll she and her friends had conducted on the question, "Should Negro students attend our high school?" The tally was: 45 opposed, 30 undecided, 85 in favor. Speaking for the majority of the school, Angie said, "We think it is only fair that the Negroes be permitted to attend this high school. . . . Have you thought what you make those Negro children feel like, running them out of school?" Angie bravely stood off angry questioners, and the meeting broke up without taking any immediate action, but Angie remained its heroine. Why did she do what she did? "Someone had to speak up," she explained; "I just don't think segregation is a Christian thing." It happens that Angie is a Methodist, but she probably had no idea that she was also a modern version of the prophet Amos in the Bible.[2]

A series of questions or comments can help to keep in focus our reflection on this incident.

1. Why should the action described be used to illustrate a high school student's involvement in mission? It seems like an example of Christian obedience or faithfulness.

That is precisely one reason it *is* used. "Involvement in mission" encompasses certain more traditional terms; another term would be Christian calling. The term need not be interpreted to suggest that some radical difference in behavior is now to be sought, nor even that a special, limited kind of Christian action qualifies as "mission." There is a comprehensiveness about the term, an urgency about it, a suggestion that our ministry is a way of entering into and carrying out our commission as God's people. These are what characterize the term as it has become a contemporary emphasis in the life of the church. In this instance, Angie faced a crisis, and she did what seemed to be right. It was as simple as that. To this observer, what happened looks very much like participation in the ministry of reconciliation. The alternative was indifference, nonaction.

2. Angie seemed to be acting in terms of the high school situation. There is no evidence of relationship to a church-sponsored or church-initiated project or action.

And that is well and good. It is cause for rejoicing. The account sounds very much like a Christian young person being the church in the world, the scattered church, and doing it naturally.

When a person or group has to look around for some service to do, chances are that there will be a note of artificiality, even though this often can be overcome. Such seeking often leads into channels of service more extensive and more spectacular (is *that* desirable?) than spontaneous action like Angie's. Conceivably, if every Christian acted responsibly in decisive occasions of his natural ongoing life, there would be less need for social action, or for service or witness committees and projects. In the meantime, however, we have not yet reached that stage.

Perhaps we *have* reached the stage at which we can give more encouragement to individuals or groups of Christians to act where they are, without needing to refer to a church structure for everything related to need or service or witness. Take the instance of a church's family's discovery of another family's need for food and clothes for school children. Instead of helping in the emergency—which they could have done easily, because the two fathers were associated in work—they waited until the next committee meeting at the church. Days later and many committee meetings later, a little help was given, with great labor on the part of the church and great embarrassment on the part of the recipients. Though involvement in mission may require channels and group effort, there is often no necessity for cluttering complications (sometimes only an unconscious plan to get someone else to do something). Mission *may* be sharing a coke with a friend—and it would be wiser not to wait until the committee meets for that!

Even if there was no church sponsorship for Angie's particular action, there is evidence that the church was in the picture. Somewhere, sometime, Angie had learned that segregation is not a Christian thing. Somewhere she had learned how to put herself in the place of others.

It would be interesting to speculate on what else the church did or might do. May there have been a group of youth and adults who met once or twice to talk about the crisis in the school? Had there been a youth program where there was some role playing in preparation for integration? Was there an awareness of support from either a small fellowship group, or the worshiping congregation?

3. The high school situation is ecumenical.

Angie evidently did not select just Methodist friends, nor just Christians, to help in the poll. Nor did she try to direct the benefits of her action to just one group. Such an approach would have been artificial and self-defeating. Perhaps Angie did not know that she was exemplifying the church's concern for the world, and the Christian's call to act in the concrete structures of society. She was, indeed, a part of the ecumenical movement, if one can agree with the definition of participants quoted on page 27 as *"all those who care* . . . test their faith in effective expressions of it."

4. Did Angie learn anything from the experience?

Again, we can only speculate. One might assume that biblical studies about brotherhood, love, justice, became quite relevant as they spoke to the high school situation—interpreting relevant to mean alive, dynamic. There was no experiencing of Christianity as a sentimental speech-making effort to sway a crowd of adults. Skillful, intelligent, fair "legwork" was done in the poll. Others were enlisted. But in the final analysis, Angie verbalized her motivation and her interpretation of the demands of the situation.

What happened is that Angie learned the truth by doing it. Learning in this sense means appropriation of faith, deepening of faith, moving to new levels of understanding the will of God and being able to do it.

A Student Cabinet Statement in a High School

The second scene is an expression by a group of youth. Resenting the stereotyping of today's teen-agers, and constrained to seek correction of some of the social ills that caused problems among them, the Student Body Cabinet of Lincoln High School in Portland, Oregon, decided to take action. After several months of study of problems connected with being a teen-ager in today's society, the Cabinet drafted the following statement and presented it to the Portland Metropolitan Youth Commission.

Passage of civil rights laws has failed to secure equal treatment for an important minority in America. This minority is cursed, refused service, and thrown out of restaurants; rudely addressed or ignored altogether in department stores; and, because of a few hard-core individuals, is stereotyped as a wild, arrogant, thrill-seeking generation. The image of this minority must be altered. No public relations program, however complete and efficiently organized, can effectively combat black markets and justifiable accusations hurled at the group—American Teen-Agers.

We of the Lincoln High School Executive Cabinet wholly recognize the shortcomings of some of our fellow teen-agers and do not condone them. Those factors, however, which have produced our generation of pressure-cooked, spirited, and rebellious teen-agers, cannot be overlooked nor minimized. We have analyzed these social, economic, academic and psychological factors. Consequently:

We shun parental "pushing" of students into social situations at sixth, seventh and eighth grade levels, and allowing dating long before emotional and social maturity. We heartily disapprove of parties for grade-school children, private and school sponsored, which have shown themselves as breeding ground for cliques, drinking, smoking and sexual experimentation.

We resent American businesses preying on the gullible teen-ager; we reject the concepts of department store "Hi-Board" parties, through which sixth, seventh and eighth graders may mix at social functions with 18-year-olds. We are provoked at American-manufactured teen-age dolls and similar toys which glorify dating, proms and parties for credulous little girls.

We deplore television, books, magazines and movies depicting teen-agers as immoral, impudent, thoughtless, empty-headed vandals.

We condemn country club dances and parties for grade-school students, despite alleged "good atmosphere" and "social prestige." We recognize the dangers of early snobbery and mixing of college, high school, and grade school age groups.

Though we acknowledge the necessity of stiff college admission policies, we are vexed by frequent testing, pressure for top grades, and making "name" colleges, for our parents' sake and our own.

We of the Lincoln High School Executive Cabinet hereby issue this statement of convictions, and appeal to students to assume responsibility for destructive or thoughtless actions of fellow teen-agers. We call upon parents and teachers to examine and amend social ills, local and national. As in any minority group struggle, fair treatment and respect will undoubtedly evolve slowly, and only when social injustices are recognized and rectified.[3]

Some of the comments made about Angie's stand may be made about this student council statement, but different factors, too, become evident upon reflection. *Mission may be evidenced even where there is no verbal witness on the part of Christians.*

This first comment may be expressed in a less controversial way. God is at work in his world; he is not confined to individual or corporate church action. Often the best thing a person can do is to discern in something going on God's presence and action, and then to align himself with that action. This approach has something to do with "man come of age," or with being a "worldly Christian," to use terms made familiar by Dietrich Bonhoeffer. William Stringfellow, who contends that the unique mark of the Christian is his ability to discern the Word of God in the common life of the world, calls upon the Christian to become deeply implicated in the real life of society.

But when the members of the Body disperse into and within the common life of the world, the Christian witness is secret, known only to those actually involved in and reached by the witness being made, known only in the event itself, except as it becomes known to other Christians in the particular intercessions of the Church for the world around.[4]

There may have been occasions of verbal witness in interpreting, reflecting, questioning in small groups or conversations between individuals, in a way "known only to those actually involved in and reached by the witness being made." There may not have been. An act, to be Christian, does not have to bear the label of Christian. Perhaps that is about all that can be said about conscious Christian witness in this incident. We would hope that Christian forces were at work, but we cannot know.

More can be said in general about the need for a verbal witness to relate an act to the Christian mission. Angie's case gives a clear example of this in the sense that her witness was a free verbalization of her view of the course set for a Christian. Stringfellow leaves room for verbal witness, saying that every layman must be his own apologist.

In fact, it seems defensible to suggest that even though it is not necessary nor possible to relate verbal witness to *every* act, such an expression is both appropriate and essential from time to time in a person's life. When a young person engages in some continuing service or activity, or is known to participate regularly in church worship, he may be asked questions which require him to "give reason for the faith that is in him." He may be called upon to explain continued evidences of concern for others.

George MacLeod, of Scotland, gives an example of the relationship of word and deed:

. . . out of missionary China comes the story of the evangelists who laid aside their Bibles in a famine and concentrated on issuing rice to enormous queues of starving men. It was disturbing on the first day that about every seventh suppliant, his bowl filled, demanded of the servers that they should tell him about Jesus. Better organised the next day they had a tent behind the open-air counter with the title "Evangelist" pinned to its door flap. As the

suppliants began again to say, "Sir, we would see Jesus," the
server brightly pointed them to the Evangelist's tent. But without
exception the inquirers remonstrated, "We do not want to hear
about Him from the man in the tent but from you who so costingly care."[5]

The importance of the *verbal* witness of Christians becomes
clear in such an illustration. Chapter 7, "Education and Mission,"
will develop further this relationship between the verbal and non-
verbal witness in mission.

1. The high school situation is ecumenical.

What was said about the high school situation for Angie could
here be repeated and underscored. The solidarity of Christian and
non-Christian youth in their exposure to pressures and dark powers
is observable in the Lincoln High School. Barriers were overcome
between church and world, as well as between denominations. The
need for help from the adult world is evident.

2. How was learning related to this experience?

If a young person were involved consciously as a Christian, he
would have numerous occasions to think through implications of
certain practices which the student council considered—the responsibility to act as well as to protest, and the relationship between his
belief and his conclusions on issues. In the process, his faith might
be clarified and deepened, particularly if a person of another denomination or religion challenged an ethical position. For any person, Christian or not, this *way of learning* offers unlimited opportunities. For example, consider these effects:

Intensive study, highly motivated, self-initiated, is more meaningful than prescribed learning.

Being forced to define one's position in conflict clarifies the
position, and helps one become committed to it.

Trying to write or say clearly what is involved brings one into
closer relationship with the content of the words, and thus
into the possibility of more responsible action as an outgrowth.

Dealing with open-ended concerns may promote continued involvement, in terms both of action and of awareness of what is being done and said around us.

A similar way of learning is illustrated by the experience of a group of young people in a United Church of Christ congregation in Cincinnati, Ohio. Returning home from an area retreat where they had considered youth ministry, the young people asked permission to have the morning service of worship several weeks later. In preparation for the service, they interviewed adults in the congregation with two guiding questions.

A typical interview went something like this: Question: "What do you think the youth should do for the church?" Answer: "Oh, I am not really sure—I guess they should come to church regularly and take part in programs and things like that." Question: "What do you think the church should do for the youth?" Answer: "We should make sure they have a place to meet and have parties and dances, and help them financially with trips and activities."[6]

At the service, one of the young people reported on the interview, and then said, "This is what *you* say we, the youth, want and need. This is *not* what we want! This is not youth ministry!"[7] He then proceeded to develop the concept of ministry as responsible participation. The result, according to the pastor, was that "a visibly shaken congregation" became one "determined to take seriously their church's ministry to youth and the youth's role as a ministry in the church."[8]

The possibilities for learning pointed out in connection with the high school situation can be transferred to the church context. Think what that group of young people learned about the congregation, the adults, the nature of ministry. In addition, we can see that when they took the initiative for doing something about their role as young laity, youth themselves were fulfilling a ministry to the church in calling attention to an omitted concern. Probably, had the young people been stymied rather than encouraged by adult reaction, their learning would have been negative, and the result negligible in the life of the congregation.

Opportunities for Involvement

In contrast to the youth initiative of the preceding illustration, unplanned and unrelated to church structures, we turn to a considered effort on the part of the Youth Committee—youth and adults—of Mecklenburg Presbytery in North Carolina. Their experiment, covering three weekends and two full weeks in the summer of 1966, was called "An Exploration into God and Life." Its purpose was to relate the church and the world in the lives of young people in the area.

Young people who had completed tenth, eleventh, or twelfth grades enrolled for the full time at the presbytery camp near the city of Charlotte. During the day they went to their jobs, if they had summer employment, or to summer school, or to places of voluntary service. The opportunities for involvement were listed in the publicity as follows:

City of Charlotte:
    1. Law Enforcement
    2. City Jail
    3. Juvenile Court
    4. Recorder's Court
    5. Sanitation Dept.
    6. Building Inspection Dept.
Adult Education:
    Adult Tutoring
Welfare Work:
    Work with Case Workers
Charlotte Area Fund:
    Youth to work in the anti-poverty program and in the Neighborhood Service Centers
Radio and T.V.—Newspapers:
    WBTV—Youth to work in the many jobs at the station.
    WSOC-TV—Youth to work with a News Reporter
    Charlotte News and Observer—Youth to work in advertising
        and with a News Reporter.
Church Service:
    Youth to work in Day Camps, Vacation Church Schools and

> other summer programs. Youth may also work in VCS
> programs in their own local church
>
> Other opportunities are being worked out by the committee.
> If you have other interest, LET US KNOW no later than
> May 1.[9]

At night there was discussion of the day's experiences, in addition to
lectures, recreation, and worship. Over the weekends, there was
time for more intensive study, relating the varied experiences of the
group to their faith.

Consider four questions as a way of analyzing "Opportunities
for Involvement."

1. Was the focus on service or on learning about community
problems and agencies?

On both—in relation to God. A major strength of the approach
lies in the fact that the youth in school, in paid employment, in roles
of information-seeking through visits and contacts in the community, and in service situations were *all* part of the community, and in
that community there was interaction among various groups who
were consciously seeking to relate to the lordship of Christ. The
structure itself was designed to interrelate service and learning, and
to suggest that *ordinary* activities like school and work are in themselves opportunities for involvement. The length of time available,
the separation for work and the return to the community for support and interpretation, the necessity for dealing with problems of
living together—all these things point to potentialities for an approach to youth ministry that incorporates many concerns which are
dominant today. The flexibility of the schedule and of the "program" has obvious advantages for youth in today's world.

2. How was learning related to the experience?

The preceding paragraph is an indirect answer to this question.
The pattern of learning described in the previous two illustrations is
applicable here also. In addition, it is to be observed that a kind of
laboratory situation was in operation, in which young people became actively involved in a number of firsthand experiences, which
they interpreted, evaluated, related to faith. The ability to articulate
the meaning growing out of the experience itself is of prime impor-

tance for whatever understanding may emerge, and for whatever direction may be set for future action.

This last point—future action—has special significance to both continuing service and learning. In this experiment, youth became involved in ways they did not want to cut off. One boy, for example, felt he must continue working with the children of a community center. Horrified at the lack of equipment and resources, he sought and received the help of his own more affluent church. Of course members of his church profited from the experience of having their eyes opened by one of their own young members. Numerous illustrations could be given of the natural outgrowths of the experiment.

3. What was the role of the adults?

Planning and preparation for the undertaking were joint youth-adult responsibilities. Adults served as resources (in lectures, discussions, conversations) throughout, but always using an approach of dialogue, of mutual concern and support, of sharing in the raising of questions and working toward answers. Adults represented the structure of the institutional church in encouraging youth to venture forth in a variety of ways. Later, in following through on the experiment, the adult community provided support through the participation both of adult leaders representing the presbytery and of congregations from which the young people came. In at least two instances families became involved in continuing service to the community center.

4. Was the experiment ecumenical?

It was initiated by one denomination, and in that sense was not ecumenical. But contacts and experiences demonstrated that broadening horizons, concerns, and cooperative ventures are inevitable if the church is to be effective in its ministry.

Another church-sponsored summer venture illustrates what can be done on a stay-at-home basis. The First Presbyterian Church and St. Paul's Episcopal Church in Winston-Salem, North Carolina, planned jointly for their 1966 summer program, which they called F.L.O.P. (For Love of People). They combined work with the city recreation department, in which they concentrated on handicapped children, and the Meals-on-Wheels program for shut-ins. In addition, they had a variety of discussion groups, centering on their work, on movies, on analyzing folk music, and the like. This was a two-month program for youth entering ninth grade through high school graduates. Such a plan demonstrated a rather dramatic shift in summer program, bringing in both the ecumenical and the service notes, but continuing the customary recreation, worship, and varied approaches to study.

Both these church-sponsored ventures indicate ways in which the church is seeking to involve youth in the ministry of reconciliation.

Other issues for analysis could be raised in all these "scenes of ministry," but perhaps the ones mentioned will point to certain key factors in the shape of work with young laity which is emerging. No final pronouncement can be given on whether these do, indeed, illustrate involvement in mission—but surely the possibility is present.

The issues which have been raised can in no way be interpreted as evaluation. The comments speculate on potentialities. The ongoing youth ministry should be characterized by analysis of specific events—failures which brought unanticipated opportunities for learning, unexpected but meaningful response to new events. Perhaps the general comments and questions considered here will offer suggestions as to how a group or a person may reflect on ventures in order to learn and to serve more effectively.

5
Where Mission Takes Place

Go to New York City and in a veterans' hospital there you will find a teen-age boy named George. He used to belong to a notorious gang of street prowlers named the Saxons. Then someone gave him a chance to donate his time to helping patients at the hospital.

. . . So George will kid the patients into doing things for themselves, and even give some a feeling of accomplishment like the college graduate who gets to help George with his math! . . .

Go to Louisville, Kentucky, and there you'll find high school students pouring concrete blocks with fancy designs on them to build a "tot lot" wall. They sit around for a while in the afternoon and discuss social problems, then the same teen-agers go home with a new sense of what Christianity is all about. Some of them who have never taken a book seriously have started studying.

In Boston a United Community Service project enlists 4,300 youth for 106 agencies. These youth may skin rabbits for medical research, or set women's hairdos in the state mental hospital.

In San Francisco 65,219 hours were contributed by 946 high school students. Because of their work thirty-five thousand children learned to swim during a recent summer.

In Minnesota teen-agers organized a recreation center for the Chippewa Indians and cut into the crime wave of the unemployed youths so drastically that the county sheriff was amazed.

In Chicago a teen-ager got interested in social projects, graduated from college, and enlisted fifty-seven students to help tutor the dropouts in the Negro Lownsdale area where 75 per cent of the teen-agers are school dropouts.

In Tennessee a young person decided to give his life to helping handicapped children after he served in a camp for retarded children for a summer.

In New York a teen-ager in the slum area has dedicated his talents in crafts to help organize a shop for boys who otherwise have nothing to do with their spare time.

On and on they go . . .[1]

Obviously, evidence of participation in mission can be found *anywhere*. The place is not determinative any more than the form or the label. Where Christian love is operative, where unpretentious service is offered, where barriers are broken down and reconciliation effected, the probability is that at least some youth have heard and responded to God's activity in reconciling the world to himself. Nevertheless, a look in terms of opportunities and problems at some of the places where teen-agers are most characteristically present may be helpful in seeing concrete forms which involvement in mission can take.

Home

Most often emphasis is on ministry *to* youth, not ministry *by* youth to other members of the family, nor *with* youth to persons and areas of need in the community. Few chasms are deeper in contemporary American life than that between adults and teen-agers, particularly parents and teen-agers; it is a chasm which cannot be crossed by adults alone. Is it totally beyond the realm of reason to suppose that teen-agers themselves *are* capable of assuming initiative in reaching out, building bridges of understanding?

Youth studies and discussions in the area of family life may well leave the "youth gripes" approach and move to consideration of ways of assuming responsibility and ministry within the family. The use of case studies or informal drama can stimulate thinking rather than focus on the private lives of families of youth.

Two illustrations are offered of approaches through study toward helping young and middle adolescents understand parents and the value of the Christian home. These illustrations are taken from study books in the Covenant Life Curriculum, a series in use in a group of Protestant denominations. Teachers of youth, in using such materials, can encourage a ministry by youth in the home situation.

William Fogleman suggests a way of beginning from the youth angle in *I Live in the World,* a text addressed to seventh and eighth graders.

> Christian parents generally want to share the life of youth in their homes, but they do not always know how to go about it. Look at the following openings for conversation ....
>
> "Dad, did you ever ——————————? Tell me about how you felt."
>
> "Mom, I think I'd like to ——————————. Would your mother let you do that when you were my age?"
>
> If you had a person whom you knew you could trust, who had done a great deal for you, who wanted the very best for you in life, and who always loved you no matter what you did, wouldn't you go to him with many questions and concerns?[2]

Few things would be more rewarding or more stimulating than for young people to ask questions of their parents, questions about faith and ethics as well as those seeking information or opening doors for communication. Lewis Sherrill, in his *The Rise of Christian Education,* has said that the Jewish family had an adult approach of unsurpassed excellence. In that tradition, as family rituals were observed and the query was raised, "What is the meaning of this?" the adult had to rethink his faith in order to interpret it. Though it may be harder these days for youth to seek the opinion of parents, for Christian young people willing to cross barriers, here is a unique opportunity that may turn out to be a service to parents in more ways than one.

In his text *How Do You Do—And Why?,* for ninth and tenth graders, Donald Shriver takes a realistic view toward families.

> Many a toothpaste ad gives the impression that family life is a cozy, happy affair. Medicine ads lift the mask of cheerful togetherness for a moment as they reveal the hostilities and miseries of family life—only to pull the mask down again with aspirin. All

of us suspect that *other* families are happy, that ours is the exception. So we guiltily hide our troubles from our neighbors, who are hiding theirs from us.[3]

He suggests that the way to overcome these "hostilities and miseries" is to understand something of the way God works today, as he did in the family of Abraham and his sons, to bring about reconciliation.

> Let us call this secret "brokenness," for the family of which the Bible speaks is a fellowship of people whose lives are constantly broken and reshaped by the hand of God moving in their experience. In such a family the father does not boast of his success, but praises God's successes in spite of human failures; in such a family children learn that before God every human being is sometimes in the wrong; in such a family parents and children can confess their sins against each other and bow together to receive forgiveness; such a family knows the joys of reconciliation, which the "unbroken" person will never know. Such a family works out its salvation with fear and trembling, for God is at work in its midst.[4]

There is, then, an expression of mission which occurs *within* the home. Perhaps the young person can serve as a light, healing, moving the whole family toward openness to God's reshaping.

More specific suggestions about the mission of the family in outreach is suggested by Roy Fairchild in *Christians in Families,* a book addressed to families. In consideration of "Family Witness in the Community," he suggests, among other things, that youth might be invited to go in small groups to homes of adults "who have demonstrated competence in their professions and jobs and who have started to think about the Christian meaning of their work as the 'scattered church.' "[5] There they would talk about their particular occupations, maybe even arrange on-the-job visits. Would it not be possible for youth to request such opportunities? Fairchild also considers a ministry by church families to youth of the community who are in trouble. Here, too, youth might take the initiative.

In one instance, fifteen-year-old Sammy did take the initiative in his low-income neighborhood in Berkeley, California, where conditions grew increasingly bad until one teen-ager got drunk, drew a switchblade, and police had to be summoned.

> "Something had to be done," explained Sammy . . . "I asked my mother to call a community meeting at our house. I went around myself to invite everyone and nearly all the neighbors came. We asked each other, 'What can we do?' We decided to start with the younger kids. They like dressing up so we planned a Better Citizens' Parade . . . joint Clean-Up Saturday for the next week—with refreshments I bought with my paper-route money. . . . Everyone was interested by now. We tackled the city Recreation Department . . . the school began giving night extension courses on how to repair a car or build a garage."[6]

Sammy sounds like an unusual person, but this is supposed to be a true story. Perhaps it can be the role of the church and of parents to see such possibilities in teen-agers, to encourage and support them, to point out possibilities, to focus on the *mission* of the Christian family as much as it has centered in the past on the *nature* of the Christian family.

Strangely enough—and yet consistent with our reflections on "scenes of ministry" in the preceding chapter—a family with such a focus, with outgoing concern and willingness to use its own life as a means of ministry, will find new and deeper unity. The same point is made by Marguerite and Frank Fidler, two Canadian writers concerned to help families find their role in meeting the world's needs. Although no two families will develop their interest in the same way, *if* they are involved in mission they have one characteristic in common.

> Their breadth of outlook, their outreaching involvement, their lively concern with other people puts the family's own domestic problems, frustrations and crises in a different light. To pretend that tension, conflict and trouble disappear would be sheer sentimentalism, but involvement in mission does lift the family's personal and internal concerns to a higher plane.[7]

Younger adolescents as well as older ones, adults as well as children, should benefit from such "ungraded" learning and service.

The situation is a different one for youth who do not live in families, who sometimes do not know who their father is. Sometimes there is no structure for discipline, no one to care whether the boy or girl spends the night on the streets. The church will have to adapt its ministry to such youth, and in a special way, will have to offer its own life as a family matrix for their growth. But as in the case of George at the beginning of this chapter, and Sammy later on, there is always the possibility of a ministry to be performed.

Church

Reference to the church as a place where mission occurs requires a somewhat arbitrary limitation. Someone has said that wherever the Christian is, there the church is. As one sixteen-year-old boy said in a panel which was giving reactions to the church, "You can't rate the church alongside family, school, and friends as to which is more important in your life. The church goes in and through these other things or it doesn't make a lot of difference. It's bigger than they are, but also a part of them." His "theologizing" about the church makes clearer the breadth of the church's relationship to mission. For our purposes here, therefore, we shall limit the consideration to these three categories: use of church buildings or facilities for service to those outside the church; participation in the church's worship and work viewed as mission; and service to the institutional church itself. Activities initiated by the church, but occurring away from the building, are considered in other sections of this chapter.

Use of Church Buildings and Equipment in Service to Those Outside the Church

First Methodist Church of Germantown, Pennsylvania, has developed several forms of youth ministry—among them, a coffee house, tutoring for students in the high school across the street, a clearinghouse for employment for youth. According to the Reverend Jared Rardin, Associate Minister who has special responsibilities for youth, the vitality of the youth ministry is a result of the church's response to rapid community changes through which it was "forced by God or by the world or both to respond to these changes or die out."[8] Adult tutoring of high school students exposed the congregation to needs of the youth in the community. A "Sum-Teen" program of summer recreation gave birth to a coffee house, which later became the clearinghouse for Teenpower, arranging part-time and after-school jobs for youth.

The coffee house, called the Glass Door, is located in a large Sunday school room with six small rooms to the side, one with a glass door opening to the back alley. Thus the name. The atmosphere, plus the church's favorable reputation with young people, means that operation of a coffee house in the church building has been no problem. There are discussions around tables sometimes, folk music, dancing, a variety of things, with food—mostly hot dogs and sodas—served primarily by the young people. Mr. Rardin makes several illuminating comments about the Glass Door.

It is, he says, "a real way in for the kids who have no relation to the Church but come regularly to the coffee house."[9] Troublemakers at dances, for example (even necessitating the help of the police force on one occasion), were gradually drawn in to work with a committee to help plan the dances. Moreover, some of the more privileged youth of the congregation who had lost interest in the church "now come regularly to the Glass Door, and in a very real sense are on mission there."[10]

A second observation points to possibilities for deepening the understanding of faith. Such an opportunity was given in this incident in which Jeremiah X, Philadelphia's Muslim leader, was invited to speak:

He came and stated very clearly his separationist theology and sociology, and then we adults stood by amazed as Negro and white together in our coffee house rose up with one voice to refute him and to protest this kind of separation, and to declare that in our community and coffee house they had learned that integration was not only possible but indeed much to be desired. And discussion, which normally we allow fifteen minutes for, ensued for an hour and a half, and our youth fellowship never talked so earnestly about eschatology or what kind of God we could believe in than they did that night.[11]

A third most interesting observation—particularly so because the coffee house movement has often been viewed as proving the ineffectiveness of the institutional church—is Mr. Rardin's statement that "the whole coffee house venture has been, to my amazement, an affirmation of institutions." The Christian Social Concerns Commission, the Membership and Evangelism Commission, and the Education Commission were involved at some point in planning and financing. Thus, "the Glass Door is a form of ministry which has represented the response of our whole church," and even though some people protest what is being done, "the church as an institution really has aided us and stood behind us."[12]

A fourth observation underscores a point made earlier in this book. Rardin says, "Our best resource as a church in ministry with youth I think is this: that the adult life of the congregation is vital and throbbing and living."[13]

As the Germantown church continues to develop its service to the community, especially to nonchurch youth, the basis for planning is the situation itself. "We find that the world is still writing our agenda."[14]

Senior highs in the Presbyterian church in East Point, Georgia, serve the children of the surrounding community in a Saturday afternoon program at the church. Already involved with adults in a tutoring program for children in a nearby government housing project, young people originally had plans to start a library there and in another housing project. When the Office of Economic Opportunity decided to launch full-scale programs in both places, the seniors changed plans. Miss Glenda Briscoe, Director of Christian Education, writes about what happened.

They scrapped the original plan and looked for an area which was not being so well reached. They made a survey of an eight-block area around our church and found over one hundred children between the ages of four and ten. This is a transitional area, economically speaking, with many old houses being cut up into several apartments and many families with lots of children and little income moving into the neighborhood. They have now launched a Saturday afternoon program of crafts, recreation, story time, field trips, for these children. It is entirely staffed by senior highs. I meet with them to help plan, and I am on hand at the church in case something which they cannot handle arises, but other than that they are doing it themselves. We feel— all of us, youth and adults—that they are opening up for this church a new and fertile field of ministry and evangelism. This demonstrates that they themselves are able to be perceptive and flexible and that they are willing to give of themselves (and even of their Saturday afternoons!) when they feel that they are engaged in something significant.[15]

Earlier, the young people of the East Point church had decided to close down their coffee house, the "Back Door." The fellowship hall of the church had been quickly transformed each Sunday evening into a pizza and soft drink center, where entertainment and conversation were available to senior highs of the church and the community. For a while, the center served a purpose, but when it was no longer meaningful, young people decided to use their energies elsewhere. They were convinced that adult churchmen and professional staff were willing to experiment with them in various forms of life and ministry. The East Point story demonstrates the values of changing plans to meet real need, of evaluating, of flexibility in programming.

Such forms of youth ministry are not an easy way out of the problems of youth work. There is, seemingly, more joint work of adults and youth, more a sense of outgoing concern; but the regular, dependable planning and hard work is as essential to this approach, when it is effective, as to more familiar approaches. Moreover, no form is free from weaknesses. In his situation, Mr. Rardin has some questions as to whether the church youth themselves are being adequately served, whether their part in mission is the final answer to their disenchantment with the church, whether the substance of the faith always comes through. The world does write the agenda, yes, but it cannot prescribe all the forms nor the content. There must be constant evaluation by the church of what is constructed to serve, lest, again, we depend on the fad of the moment to determine the shape of ministry.

Participation in the Church's Worship and Work

There was a time when, if the saints at Jerusalem were in need, the church at Galatia or Corinth could take a collection and send a delegation to convey it, expressing personal concern while they gave direct help. It is difficult to operate in that fashion today. One cannot take a few days off and deliver food to all the hungry people in India, either for one meal or regularly. Quite aside from the physical impossibility of such a task, it would be conceivable that international economy might be upset by such an act. Our assignment today has become the complicated one of setting up appropriate structures to minister in a sprawling, needy, complex society. Then, even when structures have been found and put into operation, there is the problem of motivating people to give money and of helping them to feel personally involved with suffering throughout the world. The problem is as acute for adults as for children or youth. One pastor, reflecting on what he would have changed if he were to begin his ministry anew, had this to say:

> The first thing I would like to change would be the slowness on my part to accept the agencies and institutions of the church as the service arm of the congregation. It is a tremendous thing to be able to serve around the world through these various avenues of human betterment. I would like to have understood from the beginning, as I now do, that these are *our* institutions and agencies and that it is through them that we have the greatest opportunity to accomplish God's purpose in the world.[16]

A beginning point in meeting the specified problem is surely that of adopting some such view as this. A second step is to engage in critical self-analysis, both of the local congregation's budget and of the emphases of the agencies, to make sure that every part functions as a genuine service arm of the church. Continual reformation is necessary to *keep* the church oriented toward service, in both goals and structures. For example, any duplication of effort, structures, publications, is a detriment to witness. Most denominations today are making strenuous efforts to coordinate their activities and avoid overlapping. A third thing to do is this: to keep the congregation, including young people, informed about and involved in discussion related to the whole church's outreach through its agencies. Here is a point at which education, as well as knowledgeable planning, shows itself an integral part of mission.

For several years now, the churches have made a renewed effort to include teen-agers as young laity, recognizing that general participation in the worship and work of the congregation is the essential basis for involvement in mission. Denominational recommendations for involving youth in varied possibilities for service and action help to remind us adult members to include youth, at the same time suggesting *how* to include youth. The underlying assumption is that it is better for youth to join in with the church at work—and thus learn what it means to be a part of the church—than for them to set up separate budgets.

Youth has a specific function to play in raising questions which reflect its rebellious refusal to accept the operative plan or goals as necessarily good. The recent history of one denomination, the Presbyterian Church, U.S., provides an excellent example of this role. Year after year, the denomination's Youth Council continued to nag the church as a whole about the matter of racial inequality within the church. Each year, at Montreat, the denomination's conference grounds, the council issued statements of protest and refused to go swimming or to engage in other activities from which Negroes were excluded. Maybe what they did was not determinative—but it was a stubborn reminder.

One seventh grade Sunday school class recently insisted that their church should be an inclusive fellowship, and communicated to the visitation committee their conviction that new families should be visited and invited to join the church without respect to race.

In two different youth panels conducted in 1966, at least one member of each insisted that young people should be better informed about positions held by church officers for whom they were asked to vote. One young person said he had approached members of

his session with the request that those nominated for office should
be invited to the church parlor for one or two conversations. His
proposal was that members of the congregation could come and ask
the nominees questions about their ideas on biblical interpretation,
social issues, ecumenism, anything. He was turned down with the
reply that the plan was impractical. "But it isn't," the boy said. "To
vote when you don't know anything about the candidate is irresponsible. I'm going to try again."

Service to the Institutional Church

If the institutional church is potentially a structure directed
toward efficient and effective engagement in mission, the task of
keeping it operating and constantly in the process of renewal is in itself participation in mission. The examples mentioned in the preceding section are applicable, in which the questions and reactions of
youth, as they participate in the life of the congregation, become a
spur to reform. In addition, there is the service, often manual labor,
which youth give, all the way from substituting for the janitor when
he is away on vacation to building a parking lot or repairing toys for
the children's classrooms. A special kind of learning occurs when
commitment has been "built in" through tired muscles.

In one of the consultations held in preparation for the writing of
this book, two young people mentioned their Saturday work days at
their relatively new church as being particularly rewarding to them.
"The best thing," the boy said, "is doing things with the adults. We
are about half and half, youth and adults, and we work together, not
separately. I've become good friends with some of the men in our
congregation." "What I like best," the girl said, "is being needed,
and the fun we have."

The outcome is not always so satisfactory. One fifteen-year-old
boy, a member of a youth panel, told about the effort to serve made
by several young people in his church. "We'd been studying about
stewardship," he said, "and about our responsibility as youth to
help with our time as well as our money. We knew the Every Member Canvass season was coming up—that was why we were studying stewardship—so we went to one of the deacons we knew and
said we'd like to help—stuffing envelopes, licking stamps, visiting,

anything. He told us things were already set up, and that it would probably be more trouble than it was worth to give us anything to do. So we didn't do anything." Learning of a negative nature obviously took place in this situation, just when the door had opened to tremendous possibilities for positive learning.

Any real service to the institutional church has a part to play in mission. But this service within the institution must be balanced with the use of facilities to serve the nonchurched and with outreach beyond the building itself.

School

In each of the three consultations conducted in preparation for this book, youth were questioned about the possibility of their viewing themselves as "on mission" within the high school. And all three groups came to the same conclusion: "You are asking a *hard* thing of us."

It *is* a "hard thing"- -to ask young people, just because they are Christian, to express care, concern, understanding; to help quietly without receiving credit; to be brave enough to challenge emptiness and falseness wherever they find it, even at the risk of ostracism by friends. No wonder teen-agers were hesitant about their ability to live in such a fashion! At least they were not being hypocrites nor assuming any airs of superiority as if they were already manifesting such care.

At first in the discussion, the young people thought of mission in terms of not cheating, not lying, and other "not's." Many adults who think of themselves as theologically astute today tend to react negatively to this kind of individual pietism. The young people saw and admitted readily that a list of "do not's" was not to be equated with Christianity or with goodness. At the same time, it is worth noting that the young people regarded an individual's behavior, his ref s al to engage in certain practices, as a rather crucial form of witness in the high school. "You don't have to be stuck-up about it," they said, "or to say why you aren't doing certain things. But believe you me, when they see a church young person who does all these things, maybe even more than others just to prove he's 'in,' that fixes up Christianity."

Then they talked about ways of initiating change in certain practices, maybe working through student government. Some thought the idea a live option; others were more cautious. One girl began talking about the sorority in her school, and the hurtful practice of excluding certain persons from membership. "I worried about it," she said, "but I did nothing. Now as we've been talking, I suddenly thought—why, six of us in the sorority are in the same church. *Why* didn't we at least talk about sorority membership, about our responsibility as Christians? We could have tried, at our Sunday evening meeting, to figure out something to do, and that would have been better than what we talk about lots of times. I can't understand why I haven't thought of this kind of thing before." (At least some of the adults who were present felt that had nothing else happened than this one insight and the look on the girl's face, the meeting would have been worth the effort.)

The biggest concern to the young people was about the necessity for verbal witness. With few exceptions, they were not willing to say they could or felt they should engage in what might be called verbal evangelism.

"If you're sitting at a table talking, and something just comes up in the conversation," one said, "why, *that's* okay; you can talk about religion then." Others agreed. Some admitted learning about other denominations from such conversations. Some pointed out the importance of having some ideas about one's own denomination and one's own belief to start with. All agreed that, above all else, a denominational approach to the high school was outdated.

These conversations about verbalizing one's faith or about evangelism led naturally to the consideration of Bible clubs or such movements as Young Life which seek to link youth with evangelistic structures. The mention of Bible clubs, however, met only apathetic response.

Adults who are familiar with the flourishing Young Life movement, a nondenominational organization which directs its efforts toward the high school, working through youth leaders, will be interested in the comments by senior highs. Students from one school where Young Life is active made some penetrating criticisms. "They just want outstanding people, like athletes, and make you feel like you're nobody if you aren't important." "It's sort of like another church, separate, just for young people." In another school, where Young Life seemed to be neither a separate church nor a spectacular mass approach centering around outstanding personalities, youth felt they had more share in determining activities. Some of the adult leaders believed that cooperative endeavors with Young Life might eventuate in plans for relating the Christian community to the high school world.

The consultations, in summary, produced no new forms. The idea of viewing their world, the school, as a field for ministry evidently was somewhat new to the young people. But even from the short span of the conversations, it was evident that the young people, given time and encouragement, could have found ways, forms, for engagement in mission to the high school.

Although they recognize that each situation calls for its own tailor-made approach, both youth and adults today are eager for ideas to help stimulate their thinking about the high school. One of the most significant possibilities seems to be that of School Year Ministry Groups. Growing out of interdenominational conversations about approaches to promoting ecumenical high school encounters, the "ministry group" pattern centers around weekly and daily service by small groups of youth bound together by their commitment to work in specific areas of need—school dropouts, detention or reform schools, community and hospital centers. The sequence of steps leading up to the formation of such groups might be something like this:

Concerned youth in one school meet together, perhaps at a weekend or summer conference which may be initiated by the local ecumenical youth body; they look at themselves, at their school and community, at the claim that Christ is Lord over all of life, and conclude there is a service to be rendered.

With adult helpers, and through consultation with school and community resource persons who know where to locate areas of greatest need, youth relate their resources and talents to specific problems they have isolated.

Small groups are formed, locating their responsibility in one of the areas of need. Again with adult help, they plan to prepare themselves for service, and to include other activities in their weekly meetings for planning, evaluating, and studying.

One specific proposal is presented for the weekly meetings and ongoing planning:

Weekly, each small ministry group meets to: 1) discuss the practical aspects of their ministry (schedules, programming, training necessary, etc.); 2) share with one another their experiences, their doubts and frustrations, fears and hopes, Christian relevance or irrelevance of their work; 3) study the Bible and contemporary Christian theologians toward a further understanding of their call to be Christian laymen now. The first part of each weekly meeting may also include a speaker, film, panel-report or the like dealing with some specific aspect of the field of service (e.g., a doctor explains modern obstetrics to a group ministering in a maternity home). The second part could contain a discussion of a case study written by one of the members of the group. The final part could also include a discussion of a contemporary novel, a popular movie, or a stage play.

Two or three times in the course of the school year all ministry groups meet for a Weekend Retreat Conference—not to give business-like reports, but rather to worship, study and grow together again and again as the Christian youth of the churches in the community. At the final weekend conference (or at a summer conference), some evaluations are made and new groups and groupings are established for the coming school year.[17]

What would such an approach mean for the more traditional denominational approach? Certainly there would be some change in scheduling in the effort to relate ecumenical endeavors to denominational study which would undergird service activities.

This plan or "new form" *does* mean a revision of the individual denominational youth programs in local churches, but it *does not* exclude the on-going educational endeavor which each communion considers essential for its particular youth. One community just beginning to experiment with this plan found that this ecumenical approach at youth in ministry *has* sounded the death knell for individual church Sunday evening youth fellowships (yet, each church is thankful!)—rather, the individual church now concentrates upon solid Biblical and theological teaching endeavoring to further "equip the saints for ministry."[18]

Probably the school community stands at the top of the list of areas open for ministry to the teen-ager. The school is his world. He does not have to be "sent," because he is *there* already. The question for us adults is whether—and how—we can help him know how to be the church in that world.

The Wider Community

There is no limit to the opportunity for ministry by youth, or by youth and adults, nearby and in the wider community of the world, the area of the church's concern. It is impossible to cover all possibilities, but five categories may be suggestive for consideration.

Service Projects

Called the Parkersburg Hope Corps, a group of teen-agers in Parkersburg, West Virginia, was organized on the initiative of a high school junior to help mentally retarded children in a nearby training school. The chief thrust of the service is a Saturday recreation program, but activities broaden during the summer. For the children, the program brings benefits through contact with the outside world, friendships, learning to do things otherwise not open to them. For the young people, aside from what they learn in orientation to work with the children, the program provides a growing interest in service careers and an appreciation of the opportunity to do something "worth the time" instead of getting "bored with entertainment."[19]

Tutoring is one of the chief forms of service in these days. Methodist senior highs in Corpus Christi, Texas, were invited to tutor children at a Boys' Club in the city for six weeks in the summer. Instead of the expected 50 children, 305 showed up the first day, calling for more tutors. By the end of the summer, twenty-seven children who had not been promoted had made enough progress to be allowed to go up with their grade. Obviously, such a worthwhile service could not be dropped, so Methodist youth worked with Y-Teens, Future Teacher Clubs, and others to continue giving help throughout the year. It would be difficult to say whether students or teachers are learning more.[20]

Not all service projects "work." Take this example. "What can we do to build up attendance?" a certain youth group asked frequently. "Maybe a project would help us," suggested Mary half-heartedly. "We could think up something to do." So, while the majority of the group chatted about the latest movies, two or three decided to give toys to "some poor children" (spoken condescendingly) for Christmas. The whole group seemed interested, but they forgot to plan who would collect the toys, or how they would be repaired, or who could deliver them. The project flopped. The attendance didn't increase. And things were worse, not better, in terms of any real vitality.

Reasons for failure are obvious.

The Coffee House

Illustrating again the tendency for the high school world to follow trends set by college students or by the adult world when for some reason they strike fire, coffee houses have sprung up *outside* churches as well as in church buildings. Many people, in fact, feel that they *should* be carried on away from the church, in order more easily to minister to persons unrelated to a congregation.

The story of "The Catacomb," a coffee-house-like place in Scotland, is an interesting example.

This is a place where teenagers "hang out" in an industrial city in Scotland. It was one of the first experiments of taking the church out to meet young people where they are. Started in 1959 in a few rooms loaned by the Bathgate YMCA, it now resounds with pop music at full volume, the confusion of jive and talk in an atmosphere that is cheerful and relaxed. Young people from the several church groups behind it are on good terms with those who are, perhaps "on probation," who swagger in, or the "wise guys" with attention-provoking outfits. There are no mem-

bership dues, nothing to make anyone feel inferior, no one insist-
ing on a sermon or a little evangelism when the opportunity
might arise.

Sometimes there are discussions that generate of their own
accord. Sometimes a few newspaper clippings about a race riot,
or pictures of refugees and starving children will start questions.

One of the organizers of The Catacomb said, "Would to God
that we had more young folk who were prepared to venture as
these from Bathgate have done, to new ways of service. The
Youth Fellowship and the Church in general need a new reform-
ing spirit, which will take us all out of our ivory castles, contented,
smug and self satisfied, into the Catacombs where new life is
thriving and throbbing." Perhaps the most significant comment
came from a boy who said to a girl who belonged to one of the
church youth fellowships, "Och, dinna worry aboot that—we
dinna haud it against ye!"[21]

Wherever its location, or whatever the age of its patrons, a coffee house should not be started without "a vision that puts the mission of your church squarely in the center of your concern."[22]
Douglas Trottier, a minister related to "The Fish," a pioneering coffee house for youth in Laconia, New Hampshire, continues, "Don't
do it unless you are willing to risk gigantic failure, or even worse,
unrecognized failure."[23] In The Fish, goals and a pattern for the
coffee house venture became increasingly clear.

Gradually we saw and articulated our mission in this coffeehouse as being: (1) to provide a place and a context in which we
could "serve" persons as the New Testament charges us to do,
(2) to discover and utilize more effective means to proclaim the
good news to ears not normally tuned to listen and in ways that
would invite and not block attention, and (3) to develop skill in
dialogue (on many levels). We did not compromise the style of
our coffeehouse, but rather found ourselves developing a unique
style in our attempt to use it as a tool for evangelism.[24]

In order to carry on dialogue, workers must be trained.

> Conversation is of value. Dialogue-interaction between an articulate Christian who can listen to the halting affirmations or the eloquent frustrations of another with acceptance—is infinitely more valuable. It is our conclusion that unless the church is prepared to equip its coffeehouse personnel for the task of dialogue, it is wasting time and money which could better be invested elsewhere.[25]

Too, the question must be raised about the willingness of the sponsoring group to be ecumenical.

> The coffeehouse is not suited to a narrow denominational use. Some of our best workers have been Roman Catholics. The inter-staff ecumenical dialogue has been spirited, irenic, and productive.[26]

Other hard questions must be asked and answered, Mr. Trottier says, if a church relates itself in any significant way to a coffee house venture. Lest we be tempted to see it as an easy way to appeal to youth, any of us should anticipate requirements of hard work, planning, and careful questioning about the purpose of the undertaking in relationship to the unique purpose of the church.

Work Camps

Ecumenical work camps, especially, where students live together for a relatively long period of time—long enough to get to know one another and the community where they are at work—can show some significant accomplishments. The value to participants is probably greater than the visible external results.

Ecumenical or denominational work camps, year-long internships, plans for summers or for weekends—all can be found in what might be called the work camp movement. It has been a long-time "regular" in the service efforts of the American Friends Service Committee and other groups. Again we have an adaptation of a pattern of college ministry to high school youth. Particular modifications to the abilities and interests of the age participating can enable this form of ministry to become a valuable channel for service. Here too, however, there is a great danger that the recipients of aid will be exploited in order that work campers may learn, or feel that they have served. Handled carefully, that danger can be at least partially avoided.

The basic idea is that physical labor is combined with worship and study. Opportunities are publicized through denominational offices and through the annual catalogue of service opportunities, *Invest Your Self,* published by the Commission on Youth Service Projects, under the sponsorship of a variety of religious and service agencies.

One young person came back from work camp so enthusiastic that he carried over his newly developed concern into the fall, enlisting classmates in harvesting potato crops nearby and then helping paint the Italian mission in town. A portion of a letter from him follows.

> One thing of which our group is convinced is that the best way a Christian can grow and become assured of his faith is by working out convictions, however insignificant the work may be. Just talking, while important, is not satisfying; indeed, it is frustrating in the long run. Painting the walls of a community center may be of more value actually than attending a dozen inspirational or discussion groups about helping one's neighbors. Furthermore, we are sure that the best way to overcome prejudice is to work *with* the people against whom prejudice is exerted. Trying to do *for* people is not nearly so worthwhile as doing *with* them.[27]

Just as prejudice is often best overcome by personal acquaintance when youth are pulled together in a common enterprise of service, so ecumenical education often occurs best in that kind of setting. A German theological student, who had had long exposure to ecumenical classes with scholars and to ecumenical conversations, wrote after his participation in a World Council work camp, "Now I know what the ecumenical movement is about!"[28]

A work camp experience for tenth, eleventh, and twelfth grade graduates of First Presbyterian Church, Lubbock, Texas, indicates what can happen both to those serving, and to those being served. Miss Bettye Killgore, the Director of Christian Education, reporting on the work camp, speaks of it as a "deep and meaningful experience" to her personally. Some excerpts from her account will give a bit of the background and the nature of the work.

Our plans for this began last fall at a retreat when we talked about possible service projects and also our summer activities. We felt that in the past so much of what we had done had been self-centered that it was time we did something for someone else. Part of what they wanted to do, quite honestly, would include something of adventure as well as service; something that would help them to grow personally and as a group as well as to help someone else. They presented their purposes and plans to the session at its November meeting, and it was approved along with the request to have certain money-raising projects to raise their part of the cost of the work camp. We figured the cost would be somewhere in the neighborhood of two thousand dollars and it was, for thirty of us for seventeen days. This included all the cost of food, transportation, supplies for the Vacation Church School and our work projects at the work camp, which were paint, material for curtains, etc. . . .

We traveled by an open-bedded two-ton truck that had been loaned to us by a local agency, putting benches in the back and packing our goods and supplies underneath the benches and sitting on the benches. We also had a station wagon and a trailer to help carry our baggage. We left here on a Saturday morning, May 28, and drove to Albuquerque where we stayed in the fellowship hall of the First Presbyterian Church. From there we drove the next day all the way to Towaoc, getting there about suppertime. We were housed in an abandoned government school and did all of our work of cleaning, cooking, etc., ourselves. We were there for a two-week Vacation Church School, then left there, and on the way back came by way of the Grand Canyon as sort of a sight-seeing tour, spending the night in the church in Flagstaff and in another church in Albuquerque on the way home.[29]

The work with the Vacation Church School and the young people of the Ute Indian Reservation at Towaoc, Colorado, evidently united the youth of the Lubbock church in a deep fellowship they had not known before, as they took part in their planning, their traveling, their work and evaluating, their efforts to report and interpret something of the new significance of their own personal faith. The same thing was true of the adults who accompanied the young people and worked closely with them.

In addition to the variety of work camps mentioned here, we should note adaptations of work camps, primarily as short-term work projects, for younger teen-agers. Seventh and eighth graders, with almost an equal number of adults, have frequently enjoyed a long work day on a Saturday, sometimes in a local church project, sometimes in a retreat or conference center. Continued experimentation and evaluation will enable us to use these work-approaches to their fullest potential.

Public Structures

Some people have suggested that the Peace Corps is a development of approaches originating in the work camp idea. Whether that is true or not, it *is* true that many young people today are finding meaning for their lives in the Peace Corps, Neighborhood Youth Corps, VISTA (the domestic peace corps), and other community or government agencies. Though many of these opportunities lie in the future for teen-agers, they can be interpreted to the younger group.

An Associated Press article, "Young Lives on the Line for Others," states that this is a "generation of 'doers.' "

They see that there is not only much to be done, but they believe this is the time to do it.

Suddenly youth has a job to do, and a spirit to do it with, and they carry that spirit with them.

It is there in the assured words of a Vista youth in Colorado, in the earnest, artless way of a boy from Wisconsin, in the soft sorrow of a young girl working with the poor of Chicago's north side, and in the dreams-come-true of a small town girl bound for the peace corps.[30]

The spirit which carries older youth to government service agencies is present in younger persons, and any church could check with the community organizations about openings for high school youth. Areas have made varying use of the Economic Opportunity Act of 1964 in their War on Poverty. VISTA is open to persons eighteen or over. Participation in Operation Head Start (mostly volunteer, although some employed openings exist) is open to some high school students, for work with preschool underprivileged children. Information about and cooperation with other aspects of the War on Poverty could be helpful as teen-agers talk among themselves. Someone, for example, might need to know about the opportunities available through the Neighborhood Youth Corps, which provides full- or part-time work experience and training for young persons sixteen through twenty-one.

Such openings, of course, are and are intended to be, a service *to* youth as well as service *by* youth. When ongoing community agencies of any kind open up their work for participation by high school students, they know they are taking a long-range approach to building up concern for the welfare of people—but they know, too, that the best way to begin is by encouraging youth to express their concern in service *now*.

Social Action

Most of the things we have considered have been gestures in the direction of meeting immediate need—temporary relief in situations that could not wait for more permanent solution. But if slums could be eliminated, weekend work camps to "clean up" would not be necessary. If fathers had jobs, Thanksgiving baskets would not be necessary. So service is not and never can be an adequate replacement for social action. *Is* there a way in which teen-agers can move into this deep level of reconciliation, of healing the wounds of the world? Becoming informed helps one to know when and how to write letters to congressmen, or to people elsewhere in the power positions. Preparation for lifelong occupations that will serve society is an even more significant avenue of response to God's calling. The long-range process of thinking, receiving information, preparing, cannot be bypassed in the mature approach to mission.

Of course some young people can and do engage in significant

social action now, notably the Negro young person who deliberately
seeks to break barriers. One of the "Little Rock Nine" who finally
integrated Central High School in Little Rock, Arkansas, writes of
some of his experiences. He summarizes with these words:

> As graduation neared, it was easily observed that some of us
> were becoming very nervous from the ordeal. I think it remark-
> able that we all held up as long and as well as we did. On some of
> the students, the ordeal left a permanent scar. In a lot of cases, I
> don't think all of the parents realized the shock that the entire
> situation was to them. Only two families were directly affected
> economically by the crisis. One father was a brick mason and
> had a hard time getting work from white contractors when they
> discovered that his daughter was attending Central High. Melba
> Patillo's mother was teaching in the North Little Rock public
> school system. The school board threatened not to renew her
> teaching contract unless Melba withdrew from Central. All of
> the families were subjected to a number of prank phone calls.[31]

The teen-ager who wrote these words was engaged in the process
of changing the very structures which promote hatred and division. He was going to the roots of the problem, not dealing just with
the surface evidences of it. He was paying the price of engagement
in action, social action, which gets close to the heart of mission.

His interpretation as to why he stuck it out does not indicate
whether he is a Christian, but it does suggest what Christian mission
might call a Negro young person to do in these times, in a ministry
of reconciliation.

> When you get involved with something like this, you soon realize
> that you are never doing this for yourself—because when you
> "aid the cause" it becomes very difficult. But you really can
> never get away from the idea that this whole thing is bigger than
> just you—the individual—and that it has some universal signifi-
> cance.[32]

Social action is probably the most difficult area considered, but
its importance cannot be overemphasized.

Christian Presence

There is something frustrating, an uneasy feeling, about the consideration of a great many opportunities for service. Is it the suggestion of m¹ ch activity, the unworded hope that *some* way can be found to involve youth significantly in ministry, the concern about what else should accompany the activity and the involvement? What about the process of being a Christian in the events of life as it goes on naturally?

Reaching out for some adequate statement, one may find the term "Christian presence" a reassuring one. One can just *be,* and that in itself may serve as witness to the love of God expressed through the *being.* Sometimes nothing can be done except to stay by the side of the ones who suffer, and in that staying, to express care. Sometimes the being and the doing are so intermingled they cannot be separated. Drawing on the university world, we turn to this statement of the World Student Christian Federation for an interpretation of something which is surely basic to the whole Christian community.

> Christian presence
> —is the adventure of being in the world in the name of Christ,
>   often anonymously,
>   listening before we speak,
>   hoping that men will recognize Jesus for what he is.
> —is engagement, involvement, in the concrete structures
>   of society;
>   it is a priority: we must be there before we can see
>   our task clearly;
>   it precedes witness: it *is* witness.[33]

Where, then, does mission take place? Anywhere—because God is continually at work carrying out his purpose. What we Christians do and what we say and what we are may be caught up and used by his Spirit. When this happens, we marvel, with Paul, knowing what "earthen vessels" we are, but remembering, with him, that "the transcendent power belongs to God and not to us" (2 Cor. 4:7).

6
This Difficult Business of Helping

Really to help another person is one of the hardest things one can do. It takes thought. It takes self-discipline. It takes courage and humility. But all too often in the church it has been assumed that all it takes is good intentions.[1]

Helping *does* take more than good intentions. *This Difficult Business of Helping* is the title of a youth booklet by Alan Keith-Lucas, designed to help young people prepare themselves to help. Adults who work with youth in ministering will find the booklet valuable, and may recognize the direct applicability of much that it says to their own desire to "help" youth.

One might say, also, that *serving* is difficult, or *acting* with the hope of promoting change or reconciliation in structures and policies. Much of what is proposed in the booklet is relevant to these areas also.

If involvement in mission is to be a focal point for the church's ministry with youth, it is wise to look realistically at some of the pitfalls as well as at the possibilities in deliberately setting out to serve. We have looked at problems all the way through this book, but if we pull out of the concrete situations some basic principles and concerns, they may help us prepare ourselves for a more disciplined and more Christian ministry than we would otherwise have.

Dangers

It may seem like an exaggerated statement to say that the desire to minister or the act of ministering can be dangerous. What does it mean?

1. It means that the motivation of those who serve may be questionable or false.

Alan Keith-Lucas suggests at least four frequently-found but inadequate reasons for helping.

—The desire to be liked. We help someone else because we like to be thanked or thought of as generous. We are not really thinking of the other person but of ourselves. Even more subtle but just as dangerous is the situation in which we help people we like in the hope that they will like us back. This is particularly true of those who work with children.

—The desire to feel superior. A lot of what is thought of as "pity" is actually feeling superior to someone who is in trouble. People who talk about "poor little orphans" in our Children's Homes are not really thinking about the children. They are thinking how nice it is that they can feel sentimental about the orphans and how glad they are that they are so much luckier than the children.

—The desire to control. When we help another person, we do in a sense control him. We "fix" things for him. We offer advice. This can quite easily become being proud of how helpful we are and liking to arrange things for another's good. Many would-be helpers are bossy people.

—The desire to ease one's own conscience. This is a very strong motive. In one sense it can be good, if by conscience we mean a realization that we do not deserve what God has given us and want to share this with others. But this desire can also get in the way of real helping because we are thinking of ourselves first.[2]

Such motivation suggests that, basically, one is really helping oneself.

In contrast, consider John Calvin's view that because "we are not our own, but the Lord's," we should "abandon ourselves" and enter wholeheartedly into the service of God, ridding ourselves of those "secret pests" or that personal ambition which might distort the service.[3] Or consider the biblical quotation at the beginning of this section. In response to the God who loves us and redeems us, in response to what he has done and is doing in the world, we offer ourselves to be instruments of his reconciliation. Reviewing what motivation should be, as well as what it often is, may help us become aware of our own self-deception when we outwardly are seeking to "do good."

2. It means that other subtle temptations beset one who seeks to help.

If the helper feels self-righteous, if he takes pride in the service he renders, he may be destroying himself. He may be coming to trust in his own good acts to win him favor with God. Or he may be tempted to go through a form without giving himself in genuine caring. Where there is a direct personal relationship involved, he may dispense aid but withhold love. What happens?

> If I speak in the tongues of men and of angels, but have not love, I am a noisy gong or a clanging cymbal. And if I have prophetic powers, and understand all mysteries and all knowledge, and if I have all faith, so as to remove mountains, but have not love, I am nothing. If I give away all I have, and if I deliver my body to be burned, but have not love, I gain nothing.
>
> —1 CORINTHIANS 13:1–3

On the other hand, he may choose the easiest, most immediately rewarding thing to do. He may bypass the more indirect, impersonal approach (church budgets or political action) because of the discipline and perseverance and imagination required.

Or in looking for something significant to do, he may be blind to that which is "at home." Someone has suggested that members of work camp teams may be concerned for "the others," but not for one another. One person, coming home from a conference where "Christian presence" was the much-repeated, unifying phrase, said, "There was much talk about it but there was no 'Christian presence' in our midst. Perhaps we were reserving that for other special occasions. Some of us, however, who felt ostracized, needed such a presence."

One of the subtlest temptations of all is to call for reform in situations without ever hearing the resultant call to inner personal change and reform. William Stringfellow, speaking of college students' participation in civil rights activities as a sign of health, tells about a conference in which a group of Christian students was considering their strategy for the future. They thought of concentrating on integration of church congregations instead of limiting their efforts to such places as lunch counters.

> But then it dawned on somebody what would happen if this course of action were undertaken. If these students from integrated campus Christian groups presented themselves to local congregations and asked for membership and were accepted and thereby integration began in these congregations, why then these students would have really to become and be responsible members of the congregations, at least as long as they lived in that community. It would not be like sitting-in at a lunch counter, where you might go and demonstrate and win the right for anybody to buy a cup of coffee there . . . never necessarily have to return yourself . . . Not so in integrating congregations. There you would have to come, and demonstrate, and *stay* and enter fully into the common life of the congregation. . . . This course of action . . . might well mean that the campus groups would have to give up their own existence for the sake of the broader unity of the Church in that place. . . .
>
> The discussion stopped right there . . . . as soon as a glimpse was caught of what it might cost . . .[4]

The list of temptations is already fearsome and need not be continued. The important thing is that one should learn to recognize temptations for what they are, and to deal with them for what they are.

3. It means that the one who seeks to serve may be exploiting the recipients of aid.

A social case worker suggests that at Thanksgiving and Christmas churches have often done more harm than good with their insistence on taking groups to see families receive baskets of food or gifts. With their self-respect stripped away and their privacy invaded, families would be torn between gratitude and resentment. One person might go with a case worker to deliver the gifts, she said; the professional relationship of the family with the worker—somewhat like that between a doctor and his patient—might offer some protection and guidance. The illustration points to a multitude of possibilities of exploitation in other cases.

Need exists. Hungry people cannot wait for long-range "social action" approaches. Yet good intentions do not prevent one from hurting others. In fact, as Keith-Lucas says, "In most helping the way that one helps is just as important as the actual thing that is done."[5]

Work camps, we have said, are possible forms of ministry. Like other forms they have built-in dangers, centering around the attitude with which help is offered. The possibility of subtle exploitation makes Harvey Cox, noted writer and Harvard professor, particularly wary about weekend work camps.

> Work camps provide the best example of the clear abuse of a well-intentioned gesture. For years, religious groups have been sponsoring work camps in which high school and college students from suburban areas come to a "slum" and work, often together with the local residents, to repair and paint dilapidated property. Much is made of the cooperation engendered and of the personal relationships formed. The work camps have the advantage of bringing young people into an area they might never have seen otherwise. . . .
>
> The psychology of the week-end work camp is wrong because it perpetuates an attitude of dependency on the part of those who ought to be stimulated to protest and action; and it perpetuates an attitude of condescension in those who should be confronted by their guilt in the structural inequities of metropolis.[6]

Much of what Harvey Cox has to say about these weekend projects is not applicable to work camps in general. Every situation has to be evaluated on its own merits. What is suggested by Cox is that the best possible, least exploitative way must be found to minister in each case. For example, he tells about another approach.

> Work camps are not popular with inner-city Negroes intent on changing rather than ameliorating the ghetto situation. In

light of this unfavorable attitude, one ghetto congregation recently presented a group which proposed a week-end work camp
with a counter-suggestion. The white suburbanites were invited
to come to the inner-city for a week-end, not to do something for
the slum dwellers but to be taught by inner-city youngsters how
to engage in direct nonviolent action. After the training the two
groups were to take such action not only in the city but in the
very suburban areas from which they came . . . the response of
the inner-city Negroes was extraordinary. Confronted for the
first time with the challenge of teaching something *to* white
youngsters, and taking action in the community, many of them
disclosed a level of imagination and ability they themselves barely
knew they had.[7]

Perhaps in the final analysis we can take comfort in the fact that
God can override our errors and inadequacies. When anything is accomplished, it is through the power and presence of his Spirit, not
through our independent accomplishments.

But even with such a statement, we cannot escape. Our declarations which seem to give God the glory may be an indirect way of
seeking credit for our own humility and piosity, evidenced in the expression of dependence on God and the power of his Spirit. And
that is dangerous, too!

Benefits

To counterbalance the fears of serving that may have been built
up, we must remember the very real benefits to be derived from genuine service. When a person knows that someone cares about *him*
and when hope replaces despair, then he has been given the grace to
receive help when it is offered—a difficult thing to do, requiring
both humility and courage. And when that person moves to the
point where he is able to take the initiative for his own welfare and
that of those around him, when he sees meaning and wishes to share
it with others, then the circle has been completed. The one who has
been served has now become a servant. What may have begun as a
ministry to physical needs has gone beyond to become a ministry of
healing and reconciliation.

Those who offer help may learn a great deal factually—about welfare policies, or real estate regulations, or politics. They may learn about differences between Roman Catholics and Protestants as they labor together on some work project. They may learn more about many biblical passages as they work through to Christian convictions on issues facing them. At least, if they desire to act wisely, they must get the facts.

The other kind of learning, which is achieved partly through the factual learning but goes beneath it to changes in the self, is something which happens as a by-product, not a goal, of ministry. Love becomes more than a word. The possibility of viewing oneself as of worth arises—as in the case of the Negro youth who taught white suburbanites. The wonder and the hurt of life open one's spirit to God's presence, to the gospel, and to its meaning—appropriated by the person, as, in effect, he gives himself to be an instrument for God's work.

Even the temptations we have considered may function as opportunities. The person who is exposed to himself and his own sinfulness is being offered the possibility of being remade as, in repentance, he turns to God for forgiveness and finds healing.

But if this is to happen, it will happen within the context of the Christian community—the continuing community of the past, the present, and the future. This is the community that stands under the call and the judgment of God. This is the community in which Christians interpret to one another the meaning of God's revelation of himself. It is here, in fact, that what begins as an inferior motivation may be transformed into one which is more worthy, as Christians help one another in their efforts to perceive what is right. The process is something like what Gordon Allport calls, psychologically, the development of a religious sentiment which is "functionally autonomous."[8] Fortunately, God does not seem to demand that we begin with perfection. The fact that we do *not* is the opportunity for some of the deepest benefits to be derived from ministry.

Hints for Ministry

There may be value in some summarizing statements about ministry and how practically it is to be carried out. The principles which follow are suggested in a booklet directed to helping young people choose service opportunities wisely—since they cannot do everything—and to engage in genuine ministry in that which they do choose.

1. Servants must take into account not merely obvious needs, but perhaps-more-serious needs that underlie obvious needs. Where they can, they should seek to answer underlying needs.

2. The service offered persons in need must take into account *their* need for a sense of self-respect. Persons in need should have the freedom to do what they can to help themselves, even when they do what they can do for themselves with difficulty.

3. Servants should address chronic, persistent needs with caution, and in the awareness that to offer help and then later to withdraw it may aggravate a problem in the lives of persons served. Securing counsel from experts in the field of social welfare before inaugurating a ministry will help youth in the church to avoid mistakes in the service they offer.

4. Servants should render their service in the light of what others are doing. Much that is done in church groups duplicates what is done by community agencies. Sometimes groups in the church, operating independently, serve more obvious needs in the community and ignore others. Sometimes two or more groups in the church render service in a particular situation, without knowing that their efforts overlap. The church needs to know what is being done by community agencies, and groups within the church need to know what other groups in the church are doing.

5. The importance of a service performed is not measured in terms of hours devoted or of dollars given, but in terms of the effectiveness with which the service answers some persistent or temporary human need. Alert youth can perform many services within the limitations of their resources.[9]

A Case Study and Guidelines

To get at procedures involved in ways of operating which will give form to the attitude of concern, let us refer to a condensed story of what happened in one group, and use it as a reference point for guidelines.

Members of a youth group in a small Southern town invited a delegate to an ecumenical youth conference to report. He was a Negro college student who was able to bring back to his younger fellow-Christians of another race something of the spirit of the conference, with its focus on human need. In the period that followed the talk, the young people discussed what most urgently confronted them in their own hometown. Health and housing seemed to be the point of beginning.

Plans were made to consult the sociology professor at the college, and to secure his help in making a survey to be carried on by white and Negro high school students. The things they found were amazing.

Adult churchmen worked with them to publish their findings in the local papers, and to go in teams to talk to civic groups and church groups. Public opinion was influenced. Adults began to sit up and take notice.

In the meantime, the survey showed a lack of recreational and library facilities for Negroes in the whole county. When the Presbyterian young people looked at that problem, they realized they needed help—and called on other young people's groups in town to join them. This led to the formation of a city-wide youth council.

Youth were instrumental in seeing that milk was provided for undernourished white and Negro children throughout the year. A toy store was set up where parents could come to select toys for their children for Christmas at a minimal sum. Together they set up a Negro library. Even as they did so they recognized that the separate library was not "right," but all they felt they could do at the time was to keep before them a vision of the day when all races might share all cultural benefits.

Throughout that period, a capable adult adviser worked constantly with the youth, aiding them as they planned carefully, step by step, what action should be taken.

But that is not all. When they got the feel of "Christianity in their muscles," out visiting, collecting books, repairing toys, forming friendships across racial lines, they could not stop. Last reports were that they were working on juvenile delinquency.

Guidelines on ways to proceed in this business of helping suggest themselves immediately.

1. Young people should be encouraged to keep their eyes open for real needs to be met.

The young people in the story said, "What's wrong with our town?" Studying newspapers, talking to pastors, parents, adult friends, is a beginning way—but nothing is better than one's own *thinking*.

2. A basic step is thorough investigation of whatever problem presents itself.

The group consulted the sociology professor and made a survey. Any group should seek help where and as it is needed, appointing special committees to collect information. The investigation involves looking at the problem in the light of the "servant principles" and of finding what is the Christian approach to it.

3. Efficiency calls for deciding exactly what to do—charting out a proposal for action.

The "model" group planned newspaper publicity, appointed teams for talks, arranged for continued consultation. They made definite assignments for responsibility.

4. It is important to extend the opportunity to serve, inviting the participation of others as they are needed.

What began with a Presbyterian youth group and one visitor turned into an interracial youth project, and then into an ecumenical youth organization to support the continuation of service and of friendships.

5. The group should carry through the plans, revising them as necessary while study continues.

The particular plan in consideration produced "results"—milk, toys, a library, a youth council, work on juvenile delinquency. (Some of the difficulties, of course, have not been elaborated here—nor the especially dedicated work of some few individuals. That will have to be left to the imagination.)

6. The work should be evaluated, as to the effect on others, and on the youth in the project. There is some evidence of evaluation in the case being studied, but there are no clear procedures. Questions

to guide evaluation would doubtless include such considerations as
the following:

> Did we complete our task? Why or why not?
> If we were to start over, what would we do differently? Why?
> Did we help anyone? How did they feel about our help? How did
> we feel about the help we gave?
> Did we involve other people when they were needed?
> Will there be an outgrowth, a next-step? What?
> What have we learned about the Christian faith?
> What have we learned about understanding and meeting human
> need?
> What was our purpose? Was it accomplished?[10]

7. One avenue of service should lead into another as a youth
group develops sensitivity to needs and to un-Christian conditions
around them.

Such was the case in the story. One service led into another. Ul-
timately, in service, a Christian person or a Christian group is moving toward a way of life.

It may look difficult to develop and follow through the ministries of concern to which we are called, not just because of the in-
tricacies connected with motivation and exploitation, but also because of the hard work involved. Yet a teacher does not wait until
he can teach perfectly to begin. A witness to the gospel does not
wait until he has mastered a verbal technique that gives him confidence. There is no way to escape the hard work called for in either
case.

The attitude embodied in the following poem, one known to
most high school students, might become a challenge to adults as
well as youth. Both visionary and realistic, it encourages one to keep
struggling.

> God, though this life is but a wraith,
>   Although we know not what we use,
> Although we grope with little faith,
>   Give me the heart to fight—and lose.

Ever insurgent let me be,
    Make me more daring than devout;
From sleek contentment keep me free,
    And fill me with a buoyant doubt.

Open my eyes to visions girt
    With beauty, and with wonder lit—
But let me always see the dirt,
    And all that spawn and die in it.

Open my ears to music; let
    Me thrill with Spring's first flutes and drums—
But never let me dare forget
    The bitter ballads of the slums.

From compromise and things half-done,
    Keep me, with stern and stubborn pride.
And when, at last, the fight is won,
    God, keep me still unsatisfied.

           —LOUIS UNTERMEYER, "Prayer"

III
Equipping
Young Laity

And his gifts were that some should be apostles, some prophets, some evangelists, some pastors and teachers, for the equipment of the saints for the work of ministry, for building up the body of Christ, until we all attain to the unity of the faith and of the knowledge of the Son of God, to mature manhood, to the measure of the stature of the fulness of Christ; so that we may no longer be children, tossed to and fro and carried about with every wind of doctrine, by the cunning of men, by their craftiness in deceitful wiles. Rather, speaking the truth in love, we are to grow up in every way into him who is the head, into Christ, from whom the whole body, joined and knit together by every joint with which it is supplied, when each part is working properly, makes bodily growth and upbuilds itself in love.

—EPHESIANS 4:11–16, omitting what John A. Mackay calls "the fatal comma" after the word "saints."[1]

7

Education
and Mission

Traditionally, particularly in the Reformed branch of the church, the assumption has been that education *about* the faith has been a chief means of entry *into* the faith. There is a service of the mind, offered to God as a faithful effort to comprehend intellectually the meaning of his self-revelation. What one comes to believe operates as the basis for what one does; or, to put it another way, a biblical and theological belief system is the basis for obedient response in life. Some such understanding seems to operate as a rationale underlying the Reformed emphasis on Christian education.

Moreover, in life as a whole, the chief task of youth seems to be to become educated. He is called to be a student. He spends the major part of his waking time in school. What the church does in bringing its heritage to youth is consistent with what society does in inducting youth into its life. Thus the emphasis on education for children and youth.

In this book we have deliberately begun with mission—*that for which we are educating*—as a basis for understanding the process of equipping young laity. This approach may raise a number of questions. Does this emphasis on mission negate concern for education? What kind of approach to education is called for by the focus on mission? In addition to the informal learning that occurs naturally, what *planned* structures and procedures should the church provide in its ministry to youth?

These perplexities beset us, but they point to possibilities. The intention of this section of the book is to try to consider both perplexities and possibilities, many of them implicit in what has been presented thus far. It is hoped that in such a consideration adults who work with youth will formulate for themselves an approach to youth ministry that will enable them to venture forth in ways appropriate for their situation.

Equipping Within Mission

Perhaps the most important thing to be said here is that emphasis on mission does *not* negate concern for education. In fact, it affirms that education may occur at a deeper level just because it occurs as a *doing* that is not separated from knowing. "Real Christian education—be it ecumenical or confessional—" as Albert H. van den Heuvel says, "can only come when members of an authentic community test their traditions functionally in involvement."[1]

Where, then, and how, do youth become equipped to engage in mission as young laity? Do they simply blunder forth and "do" by trial and error? These two statements point to the beginning of an answer.

First, the process of preparing to undertake the particular task at hand is in itself an equipping.

Second, when done adequately, equipping is inseparable from learning. The measure of adequacy is the degree to which the learning-equipping process links present action of youth—
—to the way God and his people have worked in the past.
—to the present activity of God and to the Christian community's understanding of that activity.
—to the future and God's ultimate purpose for mankind.

Looking at some of the ministries suggested in chapters 4 and 5, we can find illustrations for the first statement—that preparing for a particular task is in itself equipping: high school students in their getting ready to tutor children; youth who serve in a coffee house in their training for dialogue; young people consulting a sociology professor for help in determining areas of need, or preparing for a survey; youth working on speeches to present findings and needs. The preparation for a clear-cut task motivates a person to delve into his accumulated knowledge and pull together whatever is useful, and to set about securing whatever additional information or skills he needs.

Part of the role of the adult leader in this process of preparation is to aid youth in doing five things:

1. Determining exactly what the task is.
2. Deciding what information each person needs to find out.
3. Deciding what skills (e.g., interviewing for surveys, leading recreation) he should have.
4. Making plans for the necessary research or training.
5. Following through on plans.

This kind of getting ready to undertake a specific task or ministry has an immediacy about it, and relevant learning accompanies the carrying out of plans. But if the young person is to relate what he is doing to the church's mission, and if he is to build his immediate learning into the structure of his growing belief system (his understanding of faith and life), something more is required.

The second statement, that the process of equipping may be a way of learning, suggests that particular preparation must be integrated into the broader experience of learning. Such integration may take place through "theologizing," a term frequently heard in the 1960's, which refers to the process by which people seek to interpret specific events and ideas in the light of their knowledge of God and his way of working. Whatever elementary biblical and historical understanding one has is continually expanded and clarified in relationship to new insights. Questions like these are frequently asked in the process of theologizing:

What is the meaning of this?
What does God seem to be doing in this situation?
What is he calling his people to do?
What is he calling *me* to be and to do?

The questioning is a reflective process in which a person or a group attempts to formulate an idea or articulate what it sees to be true. The formulation pulls together past, present, and future. It becomes the means by which a person appropriates the truth he sees, and incorporates that truth into the knowledge he already holds.

The role of the adult is to encourage youth to raise theological questions, to reflect with them as they seek meaning, to refer them to resources, to push them deeper with his own questions.

Unless something like this kind of equipping occurs, there is no justification for saying that it may be equated with learning. Interpretation does not just happen accidentally. It must be undertaken consciously until it becomes habitual. "Doing" is itself a means of learning. John Dewey, American educator, who has acquired the reputation of having developed the cliché "We learn by doing," would disclaim that statement when it is taken out of context. It would be more accurate to say that for Dewey learning occurs through the process of "undergoing"—the involvement of mind, will, emotion, in an understanding, experiencing, relating, of what one does.

The theologian-teacher H. Richard Niebuhr indicates that sometimes "we learn nothing by doing except the bare deed." He makes the point that reflection and action must go together.

What has been implied is the conviction that reflection and criticism form an indispensable element in all human activity, not least in the activities of the Church, but that such reflection cannot be independent of other activities, such as worship, proclamation, healing, et cetera. Reflection is never the first action, though in personal and communal life we can never go back to a moment in which action has been unmodified by reflection. Even when we prevision an act, such as worship, and reflect on what we have not yet done, the act contemplated does not grow out of the contemplation; its sources in the complex human soul are more various. Reflection precedes, accompanies and follows action but this does not make it the source or end of action. Reflection as a necessary ingredient in all activity is neither prior nor subservient to other motions of the soul. Serving these it is served by them in the service of God and neighbor or of the self. It serves them in its own way, by abstracting and relating, by discerning pattern and idea, by criticism and comparison. It is served by a will that disciplines, a love that guides, by the perception of incarnate being, by hope of fulfillment.[2]

Similarly, when youth are involved in serving, they come to understand service; when they are united with other Christians, using their different talents and speaking from different confessional backgrounds, they learn that they are members of one church, the Body of Christ. Hearing about something is no longer separated from doing and experiencing. The learning that occurs is a kind of personal transformation—and this is the kind of learning with which the church is concerned.

Most young people who are ready for ministry reach this stage from a background of nurture and worship in the home and congregation. Nevertheless, others who lack that background may enter into ministry at the first point at which they are confronted. For both those who have had much previous nurture and those who have had little, participation in the ongoing life of the church constitutes a continuing equipment for ministry.

Furthermore, it is assumed that knowledge previously acquired is renewed and enlarged in the commitment engendered in each new act of true service.

Heritage and Mission

If mission is the focal point in youth ministry, what is the place of the Christian heritage? What is the relationship of the Christian heritage to a world where change reigns supreme? Indeed, are the biblical words and theological symbols really essential for life in a "world come of age"?

These questions speak directly to some assumptions implicit in the description of the process of theologizing. There are at least three such assumptions:

1. That the God we worship and whose people we are is the God of Abraham, Isaac, and Jacob, the God and Father of our Lord Jesus Christ, the God present with us as Holy Spirit. The mission about which we are concerned is his mission. Our endeavors have no point of reference, no purpose, no clarity of vision or sense of significance aside from the understanding of that mission as presented in the Bible and interpreted by the church.

2. That if the mission in which we are engaged is the Christian mission it has its point of reference in the Christian heritage and be-

comes one means by which a person receives that heritage as the center of his own life.

3. That the process by which a person relates heritage and mission is by confessing faith in God in particular situations, and in so doing, reinterpreting the heritage and appropriating it anew.

Probably what all these complicated-sounding assumptions are saying is just that the Bible is really necessary and the church's witness to the Bible is really necessary.

But "really necessary" does not mean exactly what it has sometimes been thought to mean in the past. That is, it is not intended to suggest that one first learns the Bible and church doctrine and then enters mission. One can be caught up in the efforts of the Christian community to be faithful servants in the world even before one fully understands the biblical message. Furthermore, there is a carry-over from the obedience of the Christian community, the church, to the individual's own ability to act rightly in his own situation day by day.

So, although *at some point* intellectual comprehension of the essence of the heritage is important if mission is to be carried out and if persons are to grow in Christian faith, it need not necessarily be the beginning point. Furthermore, laity, young or old, do not need a full-fledged clericalized theological training as a prerequisite for mission or for education. The shift is toward a more functional, less formal kind of study of Christian heritage. René Maheu, Director-General of Unesco, makes a suggestive observation about education in general:

> Whereas in times gone by tradition and our heritage from the past represented the mainspring of our knowledge, our force and action, nowadays it is the present moment with its most recent innovations, and even projections into the future, that dictate what portion of our past is useful or indeed meaningful to us. It is as if time had suddenly changed its course, and effect had become cause. It looks as if youth is destined more than ever before to become the cause of History.[3]

Although suggestive, the point is not altogether applicable to the consideration of Christian heritage, for the direction of the future is intrinsically related to the biblical drama of redemption. The "really necessary" reference to the Bible and church, therefore, does retain something of what it has meant in the past:

> That heritage should be studied as having value in its own right.
> That young people must be given the opportunity to formulate for themselves their understanding of faith.
> That the church is a community of language, of interpretation, of memory and understanding, as Yale theologian James Gustafson has said. Christians must continue to use the language which has its source in the Bible, both to "transmit its meanings and values from person to person and generation to generation,"[4] and to provide a means by which a person can become identified with the Christian community. That language is to be used "within the common life of the Church," and "in interpreting and understanding general human experience as it exists outside the Church."[5]

But the direct study of heritage must be carried on with more efficiency and less repetition, in a more varied schedule than in the past, in order to provide time and opportunities for engaging in mission and theologizing about the meaning found there.

The Christian Community and Mission

"He would never have survived *nor* accomplished anything had it not been for the support of his pastor and of a small group in the church who made him aware they were indeed 'with him' in his efforts," a man said of a friend of his, a city planner who was trying to design cities to serve people. His goal, as a Christian, was to develop that kind of community pattern which would offer the maximum opportunity for the growth of persons. His awareness of the reality of Christian community was a kind of equipping which sustained him in his vocation.

More than one group has been able to do *together,* in mutual support, what they would never have undertaken as isolated individuals.

If the experience of Christian community is an undergirding factor for mission, we must ask ourselves some questions. Can we be sensitive enough to young people to communicate to them our support and interest as they make mistakes and lose heart in their efforts to minister? Can a group of young people committed to Christian discipleship so experience among themselves their organic unity in Christ that they receive something of the purpose and strength that come from being part of his Body?

The first question—about our sensitivity to youth—would be suitable for discussion by all adults with specific responsibilities for youth. Some of the suggestions in the next chapters may be helpful, but no ready-made formula is known.

The second question—that of youth's experience of Christian unity—seems to call for the presence of some Christian adult who knows the meaning of Christian community and can witness to it. The acts of common worship and regular Bible study link the community together, though these may be open as well to others outside who are being served. A common discipline worked out by the group may be valuable. Perhaps the quality of unity and concern ("see how these Christians love one another!") may in itself be an evidence of the presence of some secret quality or power. All this implies that participation in the Christian fellowship is a way of equipping for service.

One of the contemporary pioneering workers with youth is Ross Snyder, professor at Chicago Theological Seminary. Few people realize more clearly than he the importance of a supportive community for young people. As he explores the meaning of "members of one body," Ross Snyder lists some of the characteristics of what he calls "a redemptive group."

> People feel deeply.
> People communicate.
> The manufacture of meanings is going on.
> A redemptive group is an arena of decisiveness and troth.
> We experience immediacy.
> We repent—realistically.
> Existence: not word games.[6]

Note the emphasis on existence, rather than word games. (Snyder refuses to be bound by grammatical rules; he seems to try to reflect or capture reality in his choice and use of words, and to involve people with him in the effort to be authentic.) What follows is his description of a model group, including a young person's comment about church membership. It projects for us possibilities of both support and learning for youth who participate in true Christian fellowship.

> Christianity is not doctrine, but existence. Truth is not statements about relationships, but a mode of life in which such relationships are actual. We know the truth only to the degree that we participate in it. We are within the daily liturgy of creation-redemption.
>
> A group is an escape from 'spiritual' into 'worldly' religion. An escape from the purely intellectual level into depth.
>
> > "I was baptized and joined the church. But I had not felt the reality of Christian convictions, in spite of confessing them 'before God and the congregation.' I accepted the conceptions of God, love, revelation, sin, salvation, and the church, without really understanding them. Without going through the process of questioning, thinking, suffering through them. Many times I have almost given up trying to struggle through.
> >
> > "But in this group I have found others who are grappling with making Christian existence real. I have come to realize myself as a *Christian in existence,* not only as a complex of verbalisms."
>
> A group is mission tackling the world; making history, not just moaning about it. A covenanted people pioneering truth trails through a wilderness, establishing a small colony of love for mankind.[7]

Snyder tells of another young person, speaking from within such a group, who said, "God is no longer simply a past or a future reality, but a present immediacy."[8]

What these young people are talking about is a nonverbal learning that occurs through relationships, and that gives content or meaning to words like "Christian," "love," "God," "members of one body."

But sometimes the verbal witness is needed to interpret the meaning of experience. Those of us who are convinced that words, our common language, must be used to provide means by which people can identify with the Christian community, would say that we must continue to teach, to educate into heritage. Fellowship, education, ministry, thus seem to be interdependent.

Such small groups characterized by honesty, support, caring, ministering, are all too rare in our churches. Is it possible for the youth ministry to provide such an understanding and supportive relationship?

Some Questions and Comments

If mission and education are as closely related as we seem to have been saying, do we imply that mission exists for the sake of education? Or that we engage in mission in order to educate? The answer is *no*. Mission is the controlling purpose—but through God's mysterious grace, people who enter into his mission and seek to be equipped for it are enabled in the process to become what he has called them to be.

We have inadvertently made the mistake in the past, on some occasions, of taking for granted that church education would lead to involvement in mission. That is not necessarily the case. Nor does right belief necessarily lead to right action. (On second thought, it may be true that real education would have eventuated in ministry; we may only be saying that we have not done an adequate educational job.) Now, as we begin with mission and then consider education, we face different concerns. One of them is expressed by Jared Rardin, whose account of the varied and influential youth ministry of Germantown (see pages 70–72) might have appeared overwhelmingly successful.

> . . . I must register a concern and discomfort I have in all this time of transition and searching for new and relevant forms, that there is much that is right and good in the evolution of youth ministry which I've tried to describe but I fear for a certain hollowness, a relevance without substance, which may best be expressed in the question, where is the Gospel in all this?[9]

At least a partial answer to Rardin's question has been implied throughout this chapter, even throughout this book. We affirm the necessity for the worship and discipline and heritage of the Christian community. Later chapters will stress occasions for study of the Christian heritage for its own sake. As to the forms of ministry, we should remind ourselves to have limited confidence in *any* forms, old or new, in and of themselves. When we evaluate, as Rardin is doing, we shall look at forms and approaches in terms of their appropriateness for the gospel to which they point.

Moreover, there is a concern about the relationship between Christian witness and service. Wherever we turn today, we see community and government agencies engaged in service. What is the distinctive role of the church and of the Christian? The question is raised by Mlle. Veronique Laufer, who speaks from an ecumenical experience in a European movement engaged in sending small teams to places of distress, seeking to serve and to be a "Christian presence." "What is different between our kind of service and the service of many non-Christian organizations?"[10] she asks. "Does our service include witness? . . . do we really care for the people to discover Christ?"[11]

What answers can we give? We are reminded of the story about the Chinese who wanted to hear about Jesus from those "who so costingly care" (p. 57). We have suggested that verbal and non-verbal witness must undergird each other. There is a helpful insight in the book by the Scottish preacher James Stewart, *The Life and Teaching of Jesus Christ*. He suggests that the great teachings of Jesus would have been meaningless had it not been for his life and death. His life embodied and interpreted his teaching. He *was* and *is* the gospel. So with us: Mission involves word and deed, the incarnation of sacrificial love and servanthood.

In one way or another, such concerns as these keep emerging. They should emerge if we are to be faithful servants. As we try to work through our questions, theologizing takes place, and we find the possibility of transforming humanitarianism into Christian witness. And unless we *do* care that people shall discover and respond to Christ—whatever form our caring may take, as it is expressed in word and deed—we are not really engaged in mission.

8
The School and
General Education

What can the church do to undergird young laity in their ministry in the school? This first question with which this chapter deals is an important one if we take seriously the view that teen-agers are strategically placed to be the church in the school.

Does the school itself educate youth in a way that equips them for fulfillment of their Christian calling? This second question is a rather unusual approach to the long historical struggle to determine a proper relationship between religion and public education in a free, and now pluralistic, society. We cannot explore all the facets of church and state and of the relationship between church education and general education, but we can look at pertinent possibilities and developments. The following topics relate to both questions.

Preparation Within the Task

The earlier description of school year ministry groups (p. 79) includes suggestions on how groups may be structured to provide for the preparation, the support, and the engaging in ministry itself as organic parts of one expression of mission. The procedure called "equipping within mission" (p. 106) offers suggestions to youth or adults who are responsible for getting ministry groups underway and continuing to work with them. The only other point to add here is that young people should be encouraged to take the initiative in requesting guidance and tangible help from church groups to which they are related as individuals. The importance of adult response has been stressed repeatedly.

Life in Home and Church as an Undergirding Factor

Participation in the life of an obedient, ministering Christian community is basic for young laity in their growth and service. The life of the community—particularly the home—communicates values implicit within it to children and youth. Such statements may seem too obvious to be mentioned, yet sometimes the simplest, most obvious factors are most important.

Consider the home. When society itself is challenging young people to social protest and expressions of social concern, can the family bear the threats to its own inner harmony by supporting its youthful members in their efforts? In fact, can the family *instigate* action? Are pressures from parents to seek grades and popularity so strong that other concerns (like Angie's, on page 52) may be ignored? Even though the peer group is assuming greater significance during the teens, the family continues to be the foundation for meaningful living. The conversations and the planning of activities offer opportunity to maintain a contact with young people and to support them in the specifics of the decisions they make.

Parents in the home and adults in the church may unknowingly be obstacles to the participation by youth in school life as a Christian ministry. On the other hand, such ministry may become a live possibility—to the degree that adults are on pilgrimage themselves, and are willing to include youth, as well as to support them in their life in the youth world.

Specific Preparation Sponsored by the Church

Conferences focusing on the high school situation seem to be developing as a possible form of direct help from churches to their young people. The Episcopal church has been active in doing this kind of thing. One report gives details of an ecumenical high school conference held over a weekend, with twenty-nine high school juniors and seniors from the New Canaan High School, New Canaan, Connecticut, meeting with eight adults. Initiated by the Episcopal church in response to a proposal from the denominational youth office for pilot ecumenical encounters, the conference included Methodists, Presbyterians, and Congregationalists. The statement of purpose follows:

Part of our renewed effort to understand the mission of the church has led us to consider our everyday life as the place where mission must take place. The high school community is the center of everyday life and work for young churchmen. To open before young people opportunities for understanding the nature and unity of the Christian mission within the high school community, we propose pilot conferences for Christian young people who attend the same schools but belong to several denominations. The conferences will take place outside the school.

Young people and faculty members from the same school will meet together in the pilot conference to accept the challenge of the gospel and to discuss its relevance to their common life and work in the school community.[1]

The planning committee met over a three-month period to select areas of tension and themes for investigation. The assistant high school principal, who served on the planning committee and took part in the conference, helped focus the program on the "situation of floating and uncertainty" in which youth seemed to exist.

In view of the apparent conflict between contemporary values and man's need for faith, the planning committee decided to begin the conference by hearing a tape recording of *The Last Word,* by James Broughton, a modern morality play. In it a man and woman in a bar, having been told that the obliterating bombs will fall in one-half hour, spend the remaining minutes trying to salvage from their pasts some meaning, something that they may say as they face the end.

A panel of four high school students was asked to listen to the play in advance so that they could be prepared to comment upon it at the opening session. Their preparation was the only involvement of young people in the planning stage.[2]

In addition to recreation and worship, there were opportunities for small group discussions, with denominations intermixed, to consider such questions as these:

"What symbols in the play were meaningful to you?"
"What would you have said as 'the last word'?"

"What tensions in high school parallel the experiences of the characters in the play?"[3]

One of the most meaningful aspects of the conference, according to the young people, was a plenary session in which adults witnessed to their faith.

> . . . three of the adult leaders spoke briefly about times in their lives when they had faced doubt and tension and about the role that their faith had played in the tensions they faced. They spoke of specific areas—such as vocation, relationships between the sexes, and the development of a personal faith—in which the more general subject of need for faith could be seen.[4]

There was some follow-up in the churches, but perhaps the most important results took place in the high school. The assistant principal was aware of new attitudes and relationships; other young people and teachers expressed interest in attending future conferences; hopes were expressed that means could be found by which young Christians in the high school ". . . might continue to be related to one another as seekers for God."[5]

Jared Rardin, whose work with youth ministries has been mentioned previously, reports on another venture.

> . . . I learned recently from a fellow clergyman in Germantown of a conference on high school life which the Episcopalians had in our area. To this were sent delegates from each diocese—three high school students, one educator, one rector; and they lived together for a week with two or three things in mind. . . . an excellent exercise in adult-youth communication. My rector friend said that by the third day kids really learned that they were being taken seriously and then were able to open up and really say how they felt about the church and the schools . . . . One of the things that happened at this conference was a 24-hour role play of the school situation, in which people were assigned roles as principles, PTA members, parent pressure groups and so on; and the issue that was presented to them was whether or not to

have a dance at which, the last time it was held, there had been serious trouble. So the friend who told me of this conference happened to be the one who was assigned the role of the principal. He said by the end of the 24 hours he had developed a physical sensation of ulcers.[6]

One of the benefits to be derived from this kind of preparation is the recognition that easy answers are not available, and that the Christian lives in the tension of having to make the best witness possible in complex situations. Coming to understand intellectually and emotionally what is involved in the complexities of living is itself preparation of the highest order; moreover, it is learning in and of itself.

Ventures like these may prompt other ideas, designed for particular schools and communities. For example, when a church encourages its youth to take time regularly for informal discussion of specific issues facing schools they attend—as membership policies of a sorority—it is encouraging them to take school life seriously. Churches have been training Negro youth in non-violent direct action. Have churches sought to prepare young people, both white and Negro, for integration, through role play, drama, discussion of news reports in papers and on television? Have young people been invited to participate with adults in neighborhood groups which have been considering their responsibility for public school issues?

Ecumenical Encounters

Planned ecumenical encounters may well be preparation for the unplanned ecumenical encounters which are possibilities for every phase and every day of school life. Whether initiative is taken by school groups, by denominations, or by ecumenical church groups, the outgrowth should contribute to areas of youth experience other than the school.

A Special Advisory Committee on Local Ecumenical Encounter was set up to explore possibilities in this area, working with the Department of Youth Work (now the Department of Youth Ministry) of the National Council of Churches. The committee has prepared some suggestive models of ecumenical encounter, and invited local

groups to report ventures in the area. Two such models are summarized here:

Weekend Conferences and Retreats. To open before young
people opportunities for understanding the nature and unity of
the Christian mission within the high school community, weekend conferences for young people who attend the same high
school, but belong to several denominations, may be attempted.
Such conferences present the occasion for young people and
faculty members from the same school to meet together to accept
the challenge of the Gospel and to discuss its relevance to their
common life and work in the school community.

Summer Conferences. The camp and conference "movement" has met real needs and provided strong, intensive experiences in Christian study and living for youth of our individual
denominations, state or regional councils. Largely, the summer
conferences are provided by the denominations. The validity of
these conferences is not being questioned. Rather, we offer the
suggestion that there is real cause for providing summer study
conferences for youth of differing denominational, racial and
cultural bodies from within a single high school community.[7]

In addition, two other models are selected from a listing of possibilities presented by one of the members of the Special Advisory
Committee.

An ecumenical high school extra-curricular club. Coordinated through the NCCC and the Catholic Welfare Conference
or similar Roman Catholic agency and some appropriate Jewish
organization. Each agency would agree to a uniform description
to be presented to the high school principal, and perhaps to the
school board for approval.

Ecumenical film night at local theater with discussion following the showing. A local theater could be asked to advertise a
showing of a selected film, with youth invited on a paid basis. A
part of the showing would include a short filmclip issuing an
invitation to the discussion. Through prior arrangement some
soda shop or coffee house could be prepared to receive the

group. Table-talk would be stimulated by selected youth who have previewed the film and received some training to lead the discussion. The film would be chosen with ecumenical implications in mind. This could be on a sometime basis depending on advertising buildup to get attendance.[8]

Reference is made also to the International Christian Youth Exchange (ICYE), now a well-known and effective means of placing high school church youth in a home and school in another country for a year. This program affords opportunities for genuinely ecumenical experience, both for the young people involved and the communities which send or receive exchange students. A modification of the ICYE plan would be an exchange of youth from different sections of the country, to live in homes and participate in the life of groups in new environments for shorter terms than a year.

Additional suggestions from the same listing of possibilities include ecumenical elective courses, regional or national study seminars, an ecumenical drugstore booth group, and a variety of others.

Such ideas may be helpful to groups willing to experiment with forms which may be conducive to ecumenism in particular situations, forms developed in relationship to denominational programs.

General Education as Undergirding Mission

The second question posed at the beginning of this chapter introduces a difficult area to consider. The position taken here, on the question of whether the school equips youth for the fulfillment of their Christian calling, can be summarized in two statements.

It is not the function of the public schools to prepare for Christian mission, although adequate education does constitute general preparation for mission.

The knowledge and skills provided through public educative processes are essential to effective service in any area of ministry today. When general education is supplemented and interpreted by the church, it becomes part of young laity's equipment for mission.

Resources are being developed to help churches view the fields of general education from the Christian perspective. A committee has been at work under the sponsorship of the National Council of Churches projecting course materials to be published under the title "Christian Faith and Public School Learnings: The Through-the-Week Series." Beginning with the fall of 1969, resource materials of two kinds will be published in the series. There are to be five basic books for teachers and other interested adults, the first on the gospel and the others on the four general areas of science, history, society, and the person, which will interpret and supplement general education. The projected courses of study, which will include teacher's guides and pupil's books for grades one to twelve, may be used in a variety of settings, under denominational or interdenominational sponsorship.[9]

Even before these promising resources are available, conversations about school studies, in church groups, should be encouraged. Why should we not build the study of church history around school study of history? Time saved in avoiding repetition and a more natural way of suggesting the church's relation to the world are two obvious values. Imaginative thinking will discover other possibilities.

General education may contribute skills as well as knowledge to the educational work of the church. Certain skills in approaching problems, decisions, mastery of new knowledge within change—these can be carried over and used in church education and ministry. Schools are concerned to develop ways of living with change as an expected factor in life. What does this concern say to the church?

Just as God is present and active in the world generally, so he is at work in schools.

This is the other, more basic reason for saying that general education undergirds mission. The difference between general and church education is not that God is present one place rather than the other. Subject matter and purpose are different, but God is equally present. Christian education cannot be confined to a particular location. To recognize this fact and to work with positive forces which operate within schools is the responsibility of the church.

Religion and Public Education

The church in our society has no right to demand or even ask that public schools should carry out what can rightly be viewed as the church's task. Worship, Christian or confessional interpretation of heritage, commitment, Christian mission—these are concerns and responsibilities of the church, not of the school. Protestantism in particular has often relied on public education to do a substantial part of its job, often quite unaware of what it was doing. That practice is not to be commended nor encouraged for the future.

However, the church does have a responsibility to encourage schools *to do a good job of education*—its legitimate task as a public structure. One of the positive outcomes of recent Supreme Court pronouncements on Bible reading and prayers in public schools is clarification of some things the school *can* do about the teaching of religion. These words of the Supreme Court are significant:

> . . . It might well be said that one's education is not complete without a study of comparative religion or the history of religion and its relationship to the advancement of civilization. It certainly may be said that the Bible is worthy of study for its literary and historic qualities. Nothing we have said here indicates that such study of the Bible or of religion, when presented objectively as part of a secular program of education, may not be effected consistent with the First Amendment.[10]

How does a school decide what it may or may not do? According to the Supreme Court, "the purposes and primary effect" of what is done determine what is acceptable; it must neither advance nor inhibit religion. This is a summary, from a report by the Department of Church and Public Education of the National Council of Churches, of what may be considered legally appropriate for tax-supported schools to engage in:

> Given the conditions cited, which will insure that the school supported by the taxpayers shows no partiality to any religious group and lets each religion flourish according to the zeal of its adherents and the appeal of its dogma, the U.S. Supreme Court has in the *Abington* and other decisions given approving mention to many things which public schools may do. According to the Court, students in public schools may—

—study the Bible for literary qualities.

—study the Bible for historic qualities.

—use the Bible as a reference book when studying secular subjects.

—study comparative religion.

—study the history of religion.

—study the relation of religion to the advancement of civilization.

—recite historical documents, such as the Declaration of Independence, which contains references to God.

—sing officially espoused anthems which contain the composer's profession of faith in God.

—make references to God in patriotic or ceremonial occasions.

—be excused from class to permit those who wish to do so to repair to their religious sanctuary for worship or instruction.[11]

Proposals for a cooperative approach to education by church and state, such as the shared time proposals, may lead to a new day in both public and church education. It is important for the churchman to keep himself informed; it is important for the church as an institution to see that laity together discharge their responsibility in this area. If churchmen encourage schools to take advantage of new doors already open to them, they can recognize and support these new educational ventures. What then shall the churches do themselves?

> Such use of the Bible in the public schools will make all the more significant the remaining task of the churches. Within its own church school, the church teaches with entire freedom for commitment; it advocates freely its own interpretation of the facts of history and its own doctrine.[12]

Church education and public education, then, are interrelated, each with its distinctive function, each equipping young laity and each benefiting from their complementary ministry.

9
Illustrative Studies:
Scenes of Nurture

If several groups made up of competent, committed youth and adults were to give serious attention to developing a satisfactory plan for the equipment of young laity for ministry in today's world, would they arrive at the same answer? If we could anticipate unanimity, we might be able to propose an ideal or model plan. As it is, we can offer, not comprehensive, overall plans, but some possibilities, some illustrative studies for reflection and evaluation. As in the case of the scenes of ministry in chapter 4, the reason for this approach is to stimulate thought and a new alertness to opportunities. Before analyzing these possibilities, it is important to note the interdependence and interaction between mission and equipping. Though separated here for analysis, the two aspects of the overall task merge in reality.

The illustrative studies suggest several different approaches to the church's role in equipping youth. One describes experimenting with new forms, one strengthening the existing plan, one revising the role of the professional staff; other approaches are described more briefly. The illustrations are a combination of actual practices told about in consultations, of reports in journals and books, and of projected ideas. In this chapter individual cases are analyzed; recurring areas of concern are considered in the next chapter.

Experimenting with New Forms

One plan, which experiments with new forms, is first described, then analyzed. The description summarizes and gives excerpts from a booklet[1] published by the Board of Christian Education of the United Presbyterian Church in the U.S.A.

DESCRIPTION OF THE PLAN

I Was a Teen-age Communicant, a booklet written for "adults and senior highs engaged in the church's ministry with senior highs," is an imaginative account from a teen-ager's perspective of a study by a group of young people and adults and the recommendations coming from the study. One of the teen-ager reporter's early complaints was this: "When people look at me, they see a TEEN-AGER, and it keeps them from seeing ME as a MEMBER." But in the process of the study, the picture changed, and the boy moved toward becoming a respected and responsible churchman, and being so accepted.

A summary of "the plan" resulting from the study is presented here.

Organizational structure

One central committee, composed of an equal number of youth and adults, with at least one church elder, was to have the responsibility for the church's ministry with senior highs. It was to be responsible to the session, the governing body of the church, through the Christian education committee. This central committee would be a planning, coordinating, evaluating body, through which youth are involved in the regular activities of church members and in their service to the world as teen-agers.

The church's ministry with senior highs

Worship. Congregational worship was viewed as "the central act of the people of God."

Study. The proposals in this section are quoted almost in full, including in parentheses the teen-ager's comments.

- Elective study courses will be offered for six weeks each, three at a time.

     (Some will be for senior highs; some hopefully for senior highs and adults, depending on the subject.)
- Three courses will be offered each Sunday, from 5 P.M. to 7 P.M., followed by supper, if this is desired.

- Two of these courses will be offered again on Tuesdays (5 to 7), for those who cannot attend on Sunday.
- There will be at least a two-week "break," with no study courses offered between each six-week period, perhaps longer at special seasons of the year.
- A small task group for each course will work with teachers as the courses progress and will handle arrangements like publicity, enrollment, facilities, etc.
- The central committee will work with the Christian education committee to select subjects, to secure teachers, and to provide for teacher-training.

     Teachers will be selected for their qualifications in the subject matter, as well as their ability to teach.

     They will be invited for a specific course on a short-term basis but may teach again.
- *Study courses for the first six weeks:*

     (We surveyed our denomination's curriculum, *This Generation* and *Youth Kit,* and found good resources on subjects we wanted. Then we examined other lists of books and resources for additional materials.)

     1. "The Church and Poverty"

          (We found good material for this in both *This Generation* and *Youth Kit.* A sociology professor, a member of our church, agreed to teach this one.)

     2. "Genesis in the Scientific Age" (Bible study)

          (The Christian education committee recommended a sharp adult teacher who has been teaching this in one of our adult study groups.)

     3. "The Church Worships"

          (We are proposing this to be youth-adult, since worship is common to all communicants.)
- If desired, some "fun and games" activity may be included with the study events, but not to interfere with the two hours' study time.
- Three times a year there will be a *weekend conference* for all senior highs and selected adults, probably during one of the "breaks."

One weekend conference will be Bible study.
  (We're tackling Romans this year.)
Another will be on . . .
"The Church in a Revolutionary World"
  (using contemporary dramas, film, etc.).
The other will be on "Personal Youth Problems."
  (This year we're picking up a course from last year's summer conference curriculum, "Being a Christian in the High School World.")

- These programs of study will replace the Sunday senior high class and fellowship.
- Senior highs will be encouraged to enroll also in any other study program open to all communicants of the church
  (like the pastor's refresher course).

We may have tackled more than we can handle, but that was our starting program for STUDY.
  (We know we will be making adjustments as we go.)[2]

Service and witness

Ten possibilities were proposed for the first year, with others to be added if desired. The central committee was assigned responsibility for coordinating church-wide enterprises with specialized youth outreach as it would be developed through small task groups.

Evaluation

An integral part of the whole plan was to be the evaluation by those who would participate as well as by the central committee, as a basis for revising future plans.

ANALYSIS OF THE PLAN

The plan itself is stimulating. Perhaps the overall pattern is clear enough to serve as reference for analysis, directing questions and comments to four areas.

Scheduling

Many questions about Sunday morning and evening meetings of youth, currently being raised almost everywhere, have been answered decisively in the plan just considered. NOTE: "These programs of study will replace the Sunday senior high class and fellowship." Perhaps the committee had heard comments like some of those expressed by teen-agers and adult leaders in the Presbyterian Church, U.S.:

> "We should have longer periods of time for a study session, and not on Sunday morning, either, not after Saturday night. Being dressed up for church keeps you from feeling informal or ready to relax and discuss, or something . . ."
>
> "A break once in a while helps."
>
> "We keep adding on things to do, meetings to have, and never, never drop anything."

Several concerns mentioned in the comments would be answered by the proposed schedule. Note also two other features: the flexibility, and the possibilities of participation in some church-wide or adult-youth study seminars, not possible if every Sunday is regularly filled with youth activities. A rigidity based on loyalty to established patterns, almost as though they were sacrosanct in themselves, has been one of the church's great handicaps.

Consideration of more than the congregational schedule is necessary, however. What if teen-agers were to become involved in the ecumenical ministry groups proposed earlier? Study and ministry would be continued there, in structures set up outside the congregation. What if youth and adults in a congregation were to join together in a community service project? A full study schedule could easily wipe out the possibilities considered here of the alternation of involvement-reflection as an approach to service and study, often across age lines.

Scheduling, then, becomes a way of determining priorities, of achieving balance between church structures and extra-church structures, of planning time for the ministry of action as well as the privilege (and ministry) of study and worship and recreation.

Conferences and retreats

Carefully planned conferences and retreats, with opportunity for intensive consideration of clearly defined areas, are coming to play an increasingly important role. The three weekend conferences for senior highs and selected adults, proposed in the plan being considered, suggest what may be done along these lines. Some churches are experimenting with weekend study-retreats as a time for basic systematic study, and using Sunday morning for informal bull sessions. Others schedule basic study on Sunday mornings, and cover special topics in several retreats per year, instead of during the traditional Sunday evening youth meeting time. Several adult leaders have said that three or four well-planned, short-term study activities each year could become the central thrust of youth study. Everybody would be present for the whole experience, planned as an entity. Short-term, small group activities would predominate in the intervening periods.

What can be said as we reflect on this use of conferences and retreats? There are values, unquestionably: Purposes and expectations can be stated, distractions can be eliminated, intensive study can help achieve depth instead of superficiality. The list of values grows rapidly. But, as with everything, there are difficulties too. New structures, plans, arrangements for leadership and use of retreat facilities, have to be worked through anew with every venture. Continuity of group and leadership, the opportunity to interweave study with ongoing, ordinary experiences of life, are forfeited. Nonetheless, there is a potential here which the church doubtless will explore more fully in these next few years.

Adult-youth relationships

At least three values should be noted in the plan described:

Youth and adults shared responsibility at every point in planning.

A small task force worked with each teacher to take care of "arrangements." In addition to this, the task force might also have served as a planning-evaluating committee to help the teacher with the course.

Youth took the initiative in requesting a course for both youth and adults.

Subjects and teachers

Examination of the subjects dealt with shows a balance in Bible, church heritage, contemporary world concerns, and specific youth problems. Research and planning in the service and witness groups would add to the spread of subjects, as well as make a direct contribution to mission. Youth will become more involved in what they have helped plan and in what they choose, as in electives. In the plan there are shorter, more manageable units which can be covered with more sense of progress than is easily achieved in long drawn-out affairs. These features seem to be strengths.

Are there any weaknesses? The desirability of changing teachers according to their competencies in particular areas is paralleled by the possible loss of close personal relationship between youth and adults over a longer period of time. (No doubt the shorter teaching terms are more practical; it is easier to get teachers for short periods.) Similarly, shifts in groupings expose youth to different young people and adults—but it is more difficult in a short time to build a group that can give support, as people work through conflicts, dislikes, ways of learning how to think together. The third and biggest question, probably, is whether the elective plan will provide the same comprehensive coverage as the carefully planned denominational cycle of study materials. Of course it is to be noticed that the planners consulted and used the denominational materials within their own overall scheme. But the question still exists in terms of long-range policy.

Perhaps the most important single feature to be noted here is that the congregation took seriously the principle that curriculum (utilization of materials and planning of experiences within their own structures and situation) must be developed in the *particular congregation*.

Strengthening the Existing Plan

In another church, another study group ended up with quite different conclusions. They decided that schedule and structure were not their problems, but rather that they had not done a thorough job with what was to go on within and through structure and schedule. "So," they seemed to be saying, "we are not going to use up all our energies in changing forms just now. We are going to select several areas for work, as a beginning, then move on to others." They determined to try to keep constantly in mind their renewed understanding which had come from their study, that youth are young laity now in a church that exists for mission. They hoped that this understanding would permeate everything they did. Some of their decisions are recorded here.

DESCRIPTION OF THE PLAN

Worship

Although almost everyone in the church affirms the centrality of worship, many, especially young people, admit that it is not so meaningful as it should be. A task force, in conference with the minister, worked out two or three things to do immediately.

The minister agreed to provide for each family a week in advance his next Sunday's sermon topic, Scripture, hymns, and three or four questions for discussion. All families were to be encouraged to set aside one time during the week for the next six weeks to use the materials provided, probably as a part of the family council plan which had already been encouraged throughout the church.

An informal conversation was to be held from five to six each Sunday afternoon, before the snack time for the young people, when any youth or adults who would do so were encouraged to talk over the morning service with the minister—not just the content of the sermon, but the whole order of worship.

Projected for the future were work groups of youth and adults to plan with the minister for the sermon and the worship. Also, there was to be a weekend retreat on worship, to include private as well as public worship.

Congregational life

Youth were included on most church committees, but the major concern was that something be done about genuine youth participation. Consequently, two decisions were made.

The church accepted an invitation to participate in an experimental project sponsored by the regional church unit, the presbytery.[3] The first step was for committee chairmen to go to presbytery camp for a period of training in the work of their committees, and in ways of working with committees including youth. The next step was to take the young people for a period of training, and finally, to have the whole committee complete training back on home territory.

A series of ten-hour youth-adult workshops in communication was set up, designed to reach as many youth and adults in the church as possible. People had a choice as to time and location; two workshops were held at the church over a weekend period; one was at a retreat center. The workshops dealt with broad concerns, including communication between parents and teen-agers.

Organization

The youth council had stumbled along weakly, partly confused by a reorganization of church committees, partly unsure of its duties. It was felt that two things were needed: (1) clarification of responsibility and authority, and (2) help in knowing how to do tasks. For the first need, the study committee commended for review and implementation a statement of function set forth in the denominational youth manual then in use:

> The function of the youth council is to relate youth to all phases of the work of the church. It is representative of all youth. It receives information and recommendations, and channels them on to the appropriate groups. It is like a steering or coordinating committee. It is like a two-way street—from the planning committees of the study groups to the committees of the session concerned with the work of the church (committees on Christian witness, service, or home and family nurture, for example) or from these sessional committees to the planning committees of the study groups; or in terms of correlation of plans, from particular study groups back to all study groups, through the planning committees. It may submit recommendations or plans to the session's committees on the basis of expressed youth concerns.
>
> The youth council should include from each study group at

least one adult and one youth . . . Any senior-high young person
who is on a committee or subcommittee of the session should be
on the youth council. A young person should serve as chairman
of the youth council.[4]

Assuming that the basic continuing working unit among the
youth was the study group—three in this particular church, one of
seventh-eighth grade, one ninth-tenth, one eleventh-twelfth—a
young person and an adult from each group would insure a channel
of communication for all youth. The "two-way" idea is important,
with the council encouraged to take the initiative wherever it was
needed.

As to the second need, the council secured the help of an experienced churchman, a businessman, as they faltered in their efforts
to work together in the accomplishment of their task. Even though
matters like electing a secretary to record decisions and unfinished
items and like preparing an agenda in advance seems elementary,
they made a difference in the functioning of the council. After making general suggestions, the businessman offered to meet with the
council twice and to spend a period at the end of the meeting analyzing the procedures in order to develop a more efficient system of
getting work done.

Study

Since a careful consideration of schedule had resulted in an affirmation of Sunday as the best time for study, the committee
centered its attention on improving what was done on Sunday, and
on clarifying some confusion about "youth" time versus "congregational" time on Sunday evening. Two decisions were made.

1. The time for the Sunday church school was increased from
one hour to one and one-half hours. Individual study in class, committee work, planning by youth and adults, was to become a part of
the class period. It was hoped that more involvement and responsibility for youth themselves would motivate interest in regular attendance; and that, except for special individual assignments or
projects, doing "outside" work *in class* would prove more realistic
than the "remember to study your lesson for next Sunday" approach. In addition, as a first step toward securing continuity in at-

tendance, an all-out effort was made to get all parents, youth, and leaders for each study group together for an interpretation of the new plan and the purpose of the course.

2. The relationship between Sunday morning and evening, and between youth and congregational activities, was clarified. The following guidelines were determined:

> Sunday morning: Regular groups to cover a planned cycle of study of the faith and mission of the church.
>
> Sunday evening: Varied schedule, with priority given to congregational activities relating to the work of the church. Participation by youth in activities of study and service planned for communicant membership. Church calendar set four periods of one month each for this. Youth to share in planning and follow-through.
>
> Choice for remainder of evening time to be made between (a) pursuit of concerns emerging from Sunday morning study groups in small groups or as a whole; and (b) signing up to participate in elective courses based on youth booklets and on other expressed interests. Plans are to be initiated by the youth council and developed by task force groups. No course is to be over five weeks. Almost all are open to all age groups; a few are designated for special interest or work groups.

Witness and service

This, everyone agreed, was by far the weakest area. The first suggestion was to set up some projects, quickly, and get all the youth involved in at least one enterprise. The final decision was a sounder one. It was to assign priority to participation in the outreach of the whole church, with specific plans made to work with church committees on getting underway with the idea. A task force was set up to look carefully at ministry by teen-agers within the teen-age world, with interest expressed in ecumenical school year ministry groups as a possibility.

ANALYSIS OF THE PLAN

Is this group still planning too much? There is no evidence that anything has been eliminated. Is everything suggested of equal importance? What could be marked off the list as it now stands?

Inclusive as the plan is, several areas are neglected. Again and again, in their study, youth mentioned the need for help in vocational choice, and the desire for more recreation, particularly during the summer. Establishing a vocational guidance program was listed as an essential, next-on-the-list undertaking, and a committee was set up to study the materials and visit a church where a definite program was in operation. Nothing was done about recreation and nothing about another expressed interest in music.

Three strengths, at least, stand out in this second plan:

As was the case in the first plan, youth and adults are working together throughout each step.

The careful study of the whole field of youth ministry brought renewed meaning and life to forms which, themselves, were revitalized from within.

The group took seriously the necessity for regular, dependable *work,* a part of which was responsibility for equipping people to do specific tasks.

But there are at least two weaknesses:

"Mission," though set up as the focal point and approached indirectly, received the least direct attention and gave the least evidence of a significant step forward.

Although community patterns may have called for no radical change in scheduling, and although drastic change in forms is not necessarily a sign of progress, the fact remains that this group shows little openness to imaginative and potentially fruitful newer patterns.

Revising the Role of the Professional Staff

Facing a building program, one church decided to review its purpose, program, and stewardship. As a result, the church rejected the building program and, instead, adopted (1) a remodeling program, to provide a few multipurpose rooms for frequent use seven days and nights a week; (2) the addition of another staff member who would concentrate on teaching youth, along with some adult teaching; and (3) expansion of the benevolent budget. The second decision, that of revising the role of the professional staff, suggests still another pattern to examine.

DESCRIPTION OF THE PLAN

Many people in recent years have questioned whether the church is deriving the maximum benefit from pastors and other professional staff. Although the trained leaders have attempted to do an adequate job of developing volunteer leadership, their own preparation might be of more benefit in direct teaching. The church under consideration felt this to be the case. The pastor and a new staff member were to assume teaching duties for all youth and for most adult groups. Some adult groups were well on the way to teaching themselves; some were neighborhood action groups; some were "personal growth groups." Lay workers were to continue teaching children.

When the planners set up two-year groupings for youth, they found that one and one-half hour classes could be scheduled twice a week, in two three-month periods. The twelfth grade would then drop out in February to form their separate group, which would run on into summer. Afternoons and nights were utilized, as well as weekends. These were a few of the factors that influenced such a radical change in scheduling.

Increased enrollment in public schools had already forced experimentation in teaching large numbers. It had been found that a master teacher can perform functions of certain types in groups of one hundred or more, using illustrated lectures, audio-visuals, demonstration, drama, and the like. Why not try the same idea in the church? No more than fifty would be involved in any one group, according to enrollment lists of the church in question.

Small group work, with teachers trained in leading discussion, and individual work (projects, papers, reports) would be able to supplement large group work. Volunteers would work with the staff member in the groups, and as resource persons for individual work. Quite specific tasks could be assigned to small groups, and leaders be prepared directly for those tasks. The denominational curriculum cycle could serve as the basic subject material to be considered, but adaptation would be encouraged. An academic setting and atmosphere could be promoted to encourage serious study.

Service and witness groups would be able to operate throughout the year, according to particular tasks. The six-month period unscheduled for study would allow time to develop other activities of interest to youth.

Two future possibilities loomed large in the minds of planners when they made their recommendation to take what they felt would be a step in the right direction: (1) some kind of cooperative effort in Protestantism for teaching youth across denominational lines, perhaps in summer school; and (2) a cooperative effort on an interfaith basis with the public schools, perhaps a shared time arrangement.

ANALYSIS OF THE PLAN

Experiments like the one proposed here are being carried out. Other experiments are needed. Most of the strengths of the plan have been indicated in the description—resting primarily in the use of professionally trained teachers, in periods of time long enough and close enough together to accomplish more than in the traditional pattern. Volunteer leaders might respond favorably to this use of their own time. On the other hand, they might assume that clergy or professional staff was being "elevated," and that the ministry of the laity was again being treated as an empty term. The only correction for such an interpretation would be a long-range effort to keep ministry in the world as the focus of laity's responsibility, and the equipping function as the focus of the professional staff. Difficulties, not necessarily weaknesses, might be found in the technicalities of schedule and in relating such an academic program to the customary more informal and varied youth program. Other disadvantages would be sure to appear.

On the other hand, if mission is to be rooted in an informed faith, it seems imperative that a more solid educational approach be developed.

Other Possibilities

Other possibilities exist in addition to the three patterns selected to illustrate directions which might be taken in planning for nurture and instruction. Young people are taking trips together across the country or even to other nations. The combination of experiences on these study-tours may be more valuable than any of the patterns considered here. Or in some small, new congregations, young people are studying, worshiping, working, with adults throughout. The same thing is true in some churches which are experimenting with new forms in their total ministry, so that youth are members of mission-groups, of house church groups, of task force groups set up to study and plan for the future. Out of many possibilities, two additional approaches will be described here, without analysis.

"Cube Group" Plan

Developed by Henri Tani with experimental youth groups when he was director of youth work for the Evangelical and Reformed Church (now a part of the United Church of Christ), the cube group approach combines study and various activities in small, closed groups. The name "cube," Tani writes, indicates "the concept of a relationship between the persons within the group and also of the presence of God in their midst."[5]

An adaptation of Tani's plan has been developed and used by Episcopalians with encouraging results. A description of their plan will give an idea as to the essential thrust of the cube group approach, though in the original plan the cube group had a closer relation to the church school than in this modification.

Fruitful experiments are now going on with an entirely new and different concept of the structure of parish youth work; the experiments appear to have many advantages. After three or four general sessions, the young people are given the opportunity to sign up for participation in a small group (eight or ten members) for a period of approximately four months. Each small group has an adult leader, and the groups meet by turns in their members' homes. By signing up, each young person commits himself or herself to stick by the group faithfully for the stated period of time. In addition, each group seeks to involve in its life and activities two "inactive" young people who have also been assigned to it. As soon as the "inactive" ones become regular, two more "inactives" are assigned. Thus each group has a continuing evangelistic task.

At the end of four months, open meetings are again held, to which anyone may come, and then, after a complete reshuffling and reassigning, up comes another period of small, closed group meetings. Each small group is required to spend at least fifty minutes of their time during each meeting on basic curriculum courses. The rest of the time they are free to plan as they will. (Acquiring a useful skill in recreation, drama, or the use of audio-visual materials are possible areas.)[6]

The "Great Conversation"

Ross Snyder has already been mentioned as one of the pioneers in youth ministry in the mid-twentieth century. What he has written in his book *The Ministry of Meaning* opens many doors to working with youth. The quotations chosen to give a glimpse of his approach show what Snyder thinks important and where he thinks we must place our emphasis. His own language is necessary to convey his attitudes. Notice how he captures and manufactures meaning in the way he uses words and sentence structure. His general comments come first, then his proposals for what he calls the Great Conversation.

We live in the time of the creating of a new culture for a *world* history. It is now evident that the whole earth is the household of God.

So on to a mutual ministry of creating and deepening meanings.

And in contemporary forms. In the imagery and words by which *we* can decide, feel, experience, project futures, give controls to our conscience, symbolize the Holy.

There is a desperate need for such people in our time of history-making. We need to be about the enterprise.

THEREFORE I PROPOSE THAT

Leaders of church and school embark upon a vigorous program of

—talking with young people *individually* . . . in their particularity.

In more informal conversation which happens as we are available to each other, wherever we are "naturally" together.

In a *new type of purposeful Great Conversation* (see next section for illustration), which both we and the young person understand is a different and distinctive style of conversation.

That such style of conversation now be included in every design of "educational program" for young people.

—inventing various forms of intensive periods where the focus remains upon some one elemental of Christian existence. This would be with a group of young people—from 5 to 40.

A whole Sunday afternoon is one possibility.

Week-end "retreats" from Friday evening through Sunday afternoon is a tested form. Week-end Great Conversation.

Sunday (or other evening) exploration groups running for an hour and a half for at least four Sundays would be another form.

—dealing with immediate news, current issues, TV programs, movies seen, happenings in their lives currently. Also with the elementals of Christian existence, the core experiences of being fully man, and Christian.

—various forms of existence clarification that come by producing art forms that express what is stirring within a person. Painting, sculpture, meditations, photographs of revealing moments of truth, poetry, free verse.

Young people should be possessing and nurturing their own experiencings of life, their own incipient meanings. They should be *creating* culture, not just using it. And in contemporary language and context. For their own age group and for the church. Create! Create! Create!

—training experiences for adult leaders and youth to learn how to launch out in such a program. Where both adults and young people are present and learning at the same time.[7]

A better idea of his understanding of "conversation" and its purpose may be derived from the following interpretation.

MEANINGS GROW BY CONVERSATION

Between two people, five people, a whole unit of youth culture

Two Persons

The basic unit of nurturing meanings is face-to-face conversation with just one other person. This co-personal world of two people is called a dyad. If we take a ministry of meanings seriously, in every Church we will have more "man-to-man" conversations with individual young people. The greatest depth and honesty of communication is possible when just two people are talking together with level eyes. More of "invocation" ("abide with me, I will appear to you"), more confirmation of the other as person, is possible in a twosome. They need not hide so much behind crowd opinion. And each is the only expert present *on his* experiences; each the one who finally has to make sense out of his life. Each is making an *offering* (in the religious sense of that word) of his experiencings, his significant feeling, his thoughts. His offering is accompanied by the implied question—"How do you see life at this point?" Yet a good co-personal world has in it some respectful distances and differences. It is neither prying or diagnostic.

Such conversation is not an opportunity for the adult to offer advice; but is a consultation on the serious issues and undergirdings of personal life. In such conversation, the young person often lives above his ordinary level of existence. And so does the adult.

And while we have been talking of the dyad as an adult and a young person, young people are constantly performing this service for each other. Can we equip them for doing it better?

But the growing of young people of high potential and courage requires that they become part of some communication network that includes adults who are making the good try. And we adults will do a better job of shaping the future if we consult those who—knowing that they must handle the consequences of our decisions—still have fresh feeling and hopes which give them special sensitivities.

Such ministry of meaning in the local Church better first involve such conversation between the pastor and the adult working with the young people. After they have made some discoveries on how to do it, then they can pull in four or five adults (or married couples) who are both significant in the community and basically "with" and "for" young people. Such a team would experience one of life's rarest privileges as they worked through such a ministry of meanings among themselves, and with young people.

The Intimate Group of Five

The next basic group after the dyad, is a small group of five or more, who have just been inside an event together. Or who have a concern about how to interpret the meaning of current news, or some movie, play, TV show. This is an informal gathering in a home for an evening, or a whole Sunday afternoon, or at the soda fountain. Wherever they like to cluster.

But we can also conceive such a group as a way of "equipping the saints" among the young people for their ministry of meanings to their own generation. For young people are the source of sanctions for each other, and in quite normal, informal conversation they do reflect upon the problematic life puts to them, they do interpret which way lies life, they do evolve a morality of their youth culture. So to equip a group of about six with the art and resources of a ministry of meanings which they can perform would be a significant forward step in a ministry *of* and *with,* rather than to youth. The young people will want it clear that they

are not going out as self-righteous propagandists, but as concerned with mutual ministry.[8]

One of the conversational approaches which Snyder suggests is
that of "bringing up and intensifying meanings by use of metaphor."

The most encompassing function of the human mind is
metaphor and imagery.

We can comprehend anything only if we *compare it to* something we already know. Our mind is constantly doing this—using
metaphors to comprehend the yet-to-be-understood. "This is
somewhat like that other thing."

And the voltage of each of the compared experiences is
raised.

Thus also the mind organizes itself into a unity.

This constant production of metaphors is certainly basic in
all growth of meaning.

Then why not encourage, train, grow this functioning? Particularly in regard to events and powerful objects that show up in
a young person's world. "What is this like? To what would you
compare it? The 'you' is important. Don't just babble hearsay—
what you have heard others say. But reach down into *your own*
stock of vivid experience and imagery. And bring the most fitting
one up." For example,

"Compared with my parents I am . . . . –"
—a baby toad on a lily pad in the middle of the Pacific ocean
—an ant beside an elephant
—a twig of a totally different tree
—a wanderer
—any teen-ager who hasn't yet figured them out
—a lovely and glossy grape; unaware of the fact that I will
   soon be the withered raisin.

These comparisons, each written by a young person, symbolize and communicate the filled-with-complex-tensions nature
of their life with their parents, their mode of tuning into their
parents and of their parents tuning into them, the territory of

their life. A metaphor does this better than many paragraphs of explanation. Further, the young people are *present* in a metaphor in a way and fullness they cannot be present in a logical talk. An hour's conversation is too short to develop all the meaning . . . .[9]

Other illustrations of metaphors that draw on other areas of experience might be given, but perhaps the passage quoted here will encourage people to explore an approach uniquely designed for " 'equipping the saints' among the young people for their ministry of meanings to their own generation." This, we have said, is the calling of young laity.

Each of these scenes of nurture is illustrative, as were the scenes of ministry. Descriptions and evaluations in both cases indicate the necessity for holding together, in balance and unity of purpose, the two emphases which have been temporarily separated for analysis.

10
Areas of Concern

Equipping for ministry takes place in many settings, through many processes, some planned, others informal. But, just as helping is a difficult business, so is equipping. Some of the recurring areas of concern, some of the repeated questions related to the nurture-instruction responsibility, are considered briefly in this chapter.

Youth Leadership

Should there be officers for the youth of the church or for various youth groups? What does being a president do for a young person by way of equipping him for effective ministry?

Several years ago it was discovered that the prevailing organizational patterns permitted the same young person to be the center of attention as president of the youth fellowship in a local church, and as an officer in two or more organizations of youth beyond the local church. After several years of "being important," he often seemed to become dependent on his leadership role. Sometimes he was not able to return to the role of an active participant. Besides this, sometimes an incompetent person has been placed in a conspicuous position and suffered inwardly because he could not do what the position demanded. On the other hand, sometimes neither of these things happened. A young person of ability often learned how to interpret the term *leader* as *servant* and to grow as he served.

Recently the tendency has been to speak less of the youth president or officers, and to use terminology like committee chairmen, study group representatives, planning groups, steering committee or coordinating committee. This tendency may be an effort partly to focus less attention on key leaders, partly to discourage making youth organizations into separate entities. Of course change in terminology does not necessarily change concepts or attitudes. The important thing is what designated youth leaders understand their function to be, and what interpretation and support they receive from the adult community as they carry out their tasks.

Another tendency has been to spread roles of responsibility and service throughout a youth group, offering a broad scope of experiences to many instead of to a few select leaders. The intent shows concern, not only over what a person does, but over what happens to him in the doing. *The role a person plays in a group does something to him.* Adult leaders must know this and know how to work with youth in interpreting their experience and in opening new doors to them. This kind of adult guidance will have a great deal to do with developing youth who can be engaged in ministering and growing at the same time.

The approach considered here is a reminder of the necessity for adapting leadership roles according to stages of maturity across the six-year span termed youth, as well as from one individual to another. We can expect seventh graders to assume responsibility on their own level, not on a twelfth grader's level. For example, ordinarily an older teen-ager might be chairman of a coordinating committee for a year; a younger teen-ager might be chairman of a committee from a study group assigned the task of interviewing a church officer, using the list of questions prepared by the group. An older teen-ager might serve as chairman of a work group with an area to investigate over a period of several weeks; a younger teen-ager, as a reporter of conclusions reached in a study group moderated by an adult. Almost anyone reading these examples will think of exceptions—the eighth grader who was able to express a clear, significant opinion in a congregational meeting; the seventh graders who prepared and presented a skit without asking adult help but responding eagerly to their own peer leaders; the eleventh grader who floundered in approaching his chairmanship of a work group. Evidently there are no simple rules. But as an adult leader learns to take much or little initiative in varying situations, to shift his own role in relationship to the ability of an individual, he develops skill and sensitivity. He is able to rejoice in the growing independence in teen-agers, and to see their leadership roles as a means of helping them establish their identity.

Worship

Worship is primarily a response to God and a communion with him. As its by-product it assists in the equipping of the saints. We may consider worship and work as two aspects of the service of God. Worship may be seen in a broadened frame of reference in this statement from a study document prepared for the churches related to the Consultation on Church Union.

> By worship the Church intends to mean every sincere act of loving response to God, individual or corporate, elaborate or simple, private or public, in the congregation or in the world. All of a Christian's life must be expressed, tested, and offered in worship, which cannot be separated from acts of love toward one another and toward the world . . . . [The Church's ministry] includes the responsibility to encourage and train the people of God in worship, individual and corporate, and to seek to nourish the body by leading it to explore new forms and occasions . . . . the worship of Christians, alone or together, is not an adjunct to their discipleship but is central to it.[1]

Young people have frequently said that they are most aware of being members of the Body of Christ during corporate worship. Whatever the church can do to promote this sense of belonging is to be encouraged. Being informed about the meaning of the order of worship and the sacraments will help those who are present to be participating worshipers, not just spectators. How does this "being informed" occur? The preceding chapter suggested some ways in which the church can begin to discharge its responsibility "to encourage and train the people of God in worship." Instruction occasionally may be a part of the service itself. Special study courses or retreats are possibilities, particularly where consideration is given to worship in the home and to private worship—an area in which youth continue to express a need for help. Perhaps the basic approach is through the regular systematic study in the church, where people hear the story of God's relating himself to human history, and make their response in worship. In fact, wherever one starts—with worship as with mission, service, stewardship—one discovers the same basis in hearing and responding to the story of God's mighty acts.

The response of worship, then, is not just a matter of "being informed" intellectually. It is a matter of involving the whole person in celebration of God's creative and redemptive acts in man's behalf. It must be admitted that the corporate worship of our churches does not always sound this note of celebration. The renewal of the church, of which so much has been said, must also include the renewal of worship. It is only as they find in it relevance to our world, a response to God's continuing acts, that young people will be able to enter meaningfully into the worship of their congregations.

A special point should be made about music. The quick response of youth to music generally suggests that training in understanding and participating in congregational singing will be an aid to worship. According to Erik Routley, British theologian and authority on sacred music, "A hymn, basically, is an opportunity for a congregation to declare its experience and to rejoice in Christian doctrine corporately."[2] But to have integrity, the response must be made through music which has an authentic Christian ring and speaks with relevance to life.

In recent years, youth have discovered in the contemporary folk song a medium of expression and a sense of involvement with each other and with the world of which they are a part. Ross Snyder quotes the testimony of a young person about what this involvement can mean.

It picks you up off the ground. At your Youth Day at the church service when we sang folk songs, I almost broke down and cried. You got caught up in a participation of worship of God that you could really take part in—really—with your whole self without being inhibited by anything like saying your prayers and being quiet. You could just let-er-go![3]

This statement expresses the response of many young people to recent experimentation in religious music in folk song form, or in using jazz settings. It is too soon to judge the significance of such experiments. As one commentator observes, "the mere presence of jazz in church does not guarantee its renewal."[4] The young person's testimony does point to the need for relevance and involvement in music and in worship. In the same conversation another young person spoke of an experience with more conventional music. "I've sung with choirs where everyone is looking at the music and detached. Sometimes something happens. Something takes over and you become involved."[5]

Other art forms also, especially visual and dramatic arts, can enrich both worship and study. Levels of emotional involvement not open to ordinary channels of logic and intellectualizing may be approached through experience with the arts.

Genuine worship is an experience which in itself motivates people to move out in service and witness, in the alternating rhythm of worship and work, as our response to God. The task of the church is to explore and develop meaningful approaches to both public and individual worship.

Study

Why have we in the church emphasized study of biblical data and stories and doctrine? Even when we have seemed to assume that the knowledge derived from study was an end in itself, surely we must have recognized that study fundamentally is a means of educating for Christian discipleship and growth in personal Christian maturity. The position taken in this book, indirectly as well as directly, is that *understanding* the faith is an essential ingredient in being transformed by it into a life of ministry. Though study is not the only factor in understanding, it is one which can be initiated by human activity, and then caught up by the Spirit and used by him to draw the student into a living relationship. The young person enters into a history which he accepts as his own, as he understands it, and finds his identity within it.

Some of the following points have already been suggested, but may be summarized here.

1. Study which takes place in the home will ordinarily be in the form of individual preparation for more formal structured study elsewhere, or follow-through on such study. The family structure itself is more conducive to informal, occasional kinds of learning than

to a school setting. It is an ideal setting for the process of theologizing which, though related to study, is not identical with it.

2. The situational study emerging out of concerns or projects relating to mission or to committee responsibilities may eventuate in the most dynamic, relevant learning in which youth engage. It, too, calls for theologizing.

3. The one continuing provision for study of the Christian heritage comes through the more formally structured classes, or peer study groups, in or related to the church. New educational developments may lead to possible changes in schedule, particularly in coordinating public and church education, or in experiments like programmed instruction. In any case, the young person's maturing intellectual powers necessitate his having the opportunity to pull together for himself his understanding of the heritage offered to him.

4. Whether or not the activity is called study, young people at each age level need opportunity to converse among themselves informally, in the presence of trusted adults, about specific personal problems they face—cheating, dating, use of time, popularity or lack of it. Periodic discussions during a Sunday meeting time, in homes, on retreats, will supplement the more formal study of the church school and the situational study in home and committees.

5. Adult-youth groupings or ecumenical youth enterprises give promise, at least on the horizon, of offering possible fruitful study opportunities.

6. One additional point—somehow the church must find a way to encourage individuals to study at their own pace, to pursue their own questions, to become responsible for their own learning. How is this to be done? This is a concern public educators also face. We know some answers, most of which stem from the way a teacher teaches or a group motivates individual exploration, but we need to seek other answers, too.

Recreation

Is it valid to say that recreation is a means of equipping young churchmen? When recreational skills acquired by youth are used in meeting needs of mentally retarded children or institutionalized groups or delinquents of one's own age in the community, these skills obviously and quite concretely are "equipment" for ministry. With the increase of leisure time—for some groups, at least—the need for recreational opportunities and for skilled recreational leadership will increase. In view of the church's concern for a ministry to the whole person, there need be no apology for viewing recreation as a part of that ministry.

There is another side to this matter of recreation—the side that perhaps need not be called equipping. To the degree that the Christian fellowship exists, it expresses itself in the joy of being together. Recreation is not simply a means to ensnare people and draw them into that which is considered *really* important. It is not a chore to be undertaken in competition with the program of some other church. It is a good in and of itself, an expression of gratitude for human companionship. Such a celebration may happen now here, now there, with different ages and groupings and occasions in the life of the church.

But of course what happens because the Christian fellowship exists, *does* also support, does free and equip Christians for their ministry. Some of the changes that have come about in tense, self-conscious adolescents through church-planned recreation that actualizes Christian fellowship, suggest that in some situations and for some communities a great deal of planned recreation should supplement the occasional recreation adequate in other communities.

The Home

We have already looked at the home as an opportunity for mission by youth. We must consider it also as one of the chief centers for nurture of youth. The home is the place where people live out what they are, and are known for what they are; it is therefore the place where people may work through those qualities within themselves which hinder their ministry to others.

Four comments only will be offered here in addition to what has been said earlier.

1. The home can provide a dependable structure within which responsible freedom develops. No other setting is quite so suited to this task as is the home.

Adults questioned in the Lutheran study already referred to had

assumed that family life would be the most troublesome area to
youth; youth said it was the least troublesome. Adults had overes-
timated youth's irritation over parental authority.

> For they wrongly assume that youth chafe under parental re-
> strictions and press for independence of action. But youth, want-
> ing to be treated as people, are more troubled by a lack of
> communication and mutual understanding in their home. They
> want the reasoned approach that is accorded adults rather than
> the arbitrary action usually reserved for small children.[6]

True, the young people were aware of and concerned about
family disharmony and about lack of "spiritual interest" or a "unifying faith."[7] But youth are open to dependable guidance from
adults who care, and in fact desire it.

2. The church has generally held that parents have first responsibility for Christian nurture. Parents who know and understand
their responsibility must work out their own ways of fulfilling that
responsibility. They have need of an attitude or outlook which frees
them from the fear of "doing something wrong."

In a course planned for middle teens, Donald Shriver seeks to
interpret infant baptism and the parents' role in a way which speaks
of the need for dependence on the grace of God.

> Yes, we present our child for baptism, that sign of the forgive-
> ness of sins, because we put our confidence not in ourselves but in
> Jesus Christ, whom God has sent to save us from worshiping our-
> selves and to enable us to live as children of his. We are not gods
> to our child, but fellow human beings and fellow sinners, who
> need the grace of God as much as helpless infants. Thus, we
> promise to bring up our child as one who has God as his Father,
> and all our attempts to be father and mother are to be controlled
> by *his* fatherhood. We seek to rear our child in that atmosphere
> which God has established for human growth in the Lord Jesus.
> We hope for our child's obedience not merely to our will but to
> God's. We hope to correct, encourage, and guide our child in such
> a way that when he leaves our home to build a home of his own he

shall gladly confess, "The God of my fathers is God indeed, whom to serve is perfect freedom."[8]

3. The whole people of God have a role to play in undergirding parents in their responsibility for Christian nurture of their children.

The child who, in baptism, has been acknowledged as a child of the covenant enters into a life ruled by God's covenant with his people—the *whole* people as an organic unity—not just with parents individually. Therefore the baptismal vows taken by parents assume the support of the congregation, a concrete expression of "the communion of the saints" throughout the ages.

Parents who are reading this book because of their desire to fulfill their responsibility to teen-agers in their family may wonder whether that support exists. They question whether the lives of the members of their congregation embody the values they wish their children to receive, whether ideas conveyed in study have any meaning for today's youth, whether the quality of love and helping is strong enough to be experienced by younger churchmen.

On the other hand, they know that their own attitudes toward the church—their regular participation in its life, their comments around the table, their efforts to work for its renewal—help determine whether the meaning which *is* present in the church is communicated to their families.

There are concrete ways in which the church may help parents, in addition to the intangible influences just mentioned, such as youth-adult study groups, short-term discussion groups on special topics, parents' participation in the preparation of their sons and daughters for confirmation, family camping. In one United Presbyterian congregation, several senior highs were invited to meet with parents of eighth or ninth graders to talk about "things they wish their parents had done or understood when they started senior high school."[9] The idea spread and the questions were varied. In one situation, the conversation centered around parental attitudes toward junior high participation in church; in another, college students talked with parents who had seniors preparing for college, and young working adults with parents whose sons and daughters expected to be employed after high school.

A balance must be sought between risking the destruction of family life by too many church-sponsored meetings and neglecting to provide support, guidance, and help as needed. The whole area of the church's ministry to families needs careful thought. If families are to be nurturing centers, they themselves need the nurture of the whole Christian community.

4. Participation in the life of a family which is oriented toward mission is in itself equipping for a life of ministry.

Another illustration from Donald Shriver makes the point clear.

When lips had just about stopped smacking over the cherry pie, Mr. Lockhart motioned to the assembled multitude of Lockharts and said, "Have a seat, you four; your mother and I have decided to call a family council. An *advisory* council, you understand—strictly advisory."

"Sure, Dad," said fourteen-year-old Tim with a flourish. "How can I help you out?"

"Just by listening for a while, wise one. I hear a rumor that this family is protesting my long-time-no-see policy. You're jealous of that law office downtown, right?"

"Right!" came a unison reply.

"You're looking forward to our trip to Grand Canyon this August, right?"

"Right!" came a louder unison reply.

"Well, I've got something to report that you may think is not so right. As those of you who read more than the funny papers know, Kenneth Rutgers has decided to run for Congress against Fred Lawler, who has had the job for twelve years. Last year Lawler helped block appropriations for the Civil Rights Commission, and he is a leader among those politicians in the state who favor a state lottery as a source of revenue. He intends to drum up a campaign on these two issues, and Ken Rutgers has decided to run against him. Ken wants me to be his campaign manager, and that means six months of hard work between now and November—besides all the work I'm doing now. So the question is . . ."

"Whether we go on vacation or not," moaned Tim.

"Yes, I'm afraid so. And the worst of it is that some folks say Lawler can't possibly be beaten in this year's election. It may be a sacrifice for nothing. Are you game for going along with another losing cause?"

Four heads looked down at the tablecloth, at least three of them remembering how many cases their father had tried in court for people who had no money to pay him, and how only last year he had unsuccessfully led the attempt to declare their neighborhood open to all residents regardless of race. Many people had accused him of being a "no-good do-gooder."

"Well, Dad," said Tim slowly, "you know what we think. If it's worth doing, it's worth trying; and maybe we can go to the Canyon next year."

"I hope so, Tim," said Mr. Lockhart, smiling. "I'm sorry about this year."

"That's okay, Dad," said Tim. "We don't see you much, but we sure like what you're doing. Say, how about letting me help stuff envelopes again? They do stuff envelopes in election campaigns, don't they?"[10]

Individual life, family life, and church life come together in these comments and illustrations which relate to the home as an area of concern. To say this is to note again that the church's ministry with youth cannot be viewed in isolation. It takes place on many fronts, as part of a broader, inclusive ministry.

The Age for the Profession of Faith

Whether it is called confirmation, profession of faith, or by some other designation, various denominations, Catholic as well as Protestant, have a common concern about the wisest preparation and the most suitable age for the young person to take this step. This is the point in his experience when he is acknowledged by the congregation as a responsible, communing member, in the manner appropriate to the church's particular tradition, and when he accepts for himself the privileges and responsibilities of such a relationship.

Once more the polity and practice of one communion, the Presbyterian Church, U.S., will provide an illustrative example. The official Book of Church Order makes this definitive statement:

> Children born within the Church are under the care of a particular church. They are to be taught to love God, and to obey and serve the Lord Jesus Christ. When they come to years of discretion they should be earnestly reminded by parents and Church Session that they are members of the Church by birthright, and that it is their duty and privilege personally to profess before men their faith in Christ and to seek admission to the Lord's Table and enrollment as communing members in a particular church.[11]

Although "the time when young persons come to years of discretion is not precisely fixed,"[12] the pattern of life in a particular church and the expectations and curriculum materials have a great deal to do with the time a child of the covenant moves into communicant membership.

What is the present expectation in the Presbyterian Church, U.S.? A manual for pastor and session offers this answer:

> In developing the Covenant Life Curriculum, planners have posited the age of seventh and eighth graders as the age at which provision may best be made for youth to receive definite help and encouragement toward becoming communing members of the church. The basic formal experience for which provision is made in the curriculum is study of *The Church, a Believing Fellowship,* the study book by William M. Ramsay and John H. Leith used in the second of the three-year cycle of systematic study in the curriculum. The course treats the history, the faith, the forms, and the worship and work of the church. Serious study of the book should yield a comprehension of the data of the faith that may serve as the intellectual basis for decision to become a communing member.[13]

The description sounds like the content of what is usually called the communicants' class. This suggests that a second class with identical subject matter should *not* be scheduled concurrently with a church school study of *The Church, a Believing Fellowship!* Although the pastor may choose to give additional instruction, the plan also points to a new role for the session and the parents, with specially designed materials for their guidance. Elders are encouraged to establish a personal relationship with the young people contemplating communicant membership.

> . . . the task of those related to youth being oriented to communicant membership becomes, *not* primarily a matter of helping the youth gain a knowledge of the Bible and of facts relevant to the life of a communing member, *but* a matter of checking on what he should have learned in the school of the church in the years of childhood, of helping him appreciate the meaning of the experience he is having, and of introducing him to responsible membership in the church.[14]

In such a relationship, emphasis can be placed on freedom of the youth to respond individually, rather than routinely as part of a group decision. The plan is relatively new, but its possibilities seem great. Churches will experiment with it and adapt it, just as they are doing about the age when they encourage a profession of faith. Some churches are steadily moving toward an older age as a more appropriate time for that profession.

Vocational Guidance

One area in which youth need specific help against the background of the meaning of life and of the call to be a Christian is the area of finding and using their gifts in particular occupations. The Lutheran study says this: "Apparently most youth want help from the church in the areas of *vocational guidance, boy-girl relationships,* and *Christian outreach.*"[15]

If the expressed need for vocational guidance is as strong as indicated, help in this area must rank high on the priority list for churches. Though many junior and senior high schools offer help, the basis for understanding Christian vocation rests in the teachings of the church. But the relating of faith to work is the problem and the challenge.

A plan developed cooperatively through the National Council of Churches is implemented in *You and Your Lifework: A Christian Choice for Youth,* a set of materials prepared by Albert Curry Winn. Students, preferably sophomores, make use of a study-notebook in their study of vocation, self-understanding, and opportunities for choice of work. Adult leaders, sometimes called vocational aides, have a guide to supplement the guidance materials for youth. Parents also have a guide for their part of the plan.

If we take the doctrine of Christian vocation seriously, we will have to recognize that every Christian is called to full-time service. Further, we must help Christian adults to discover meaning in the job *they* now have. Is all of *this* a part of helping a young person make a choice? Yes, Winn says to those who are serving as leaders.

> We want to keep young people from deciding on their first jobs by sheer chance, as four-fifths of them reportedly do now. We want to prevent their joining the more than 50 per cent of all middle-aged adults who wish they were in a different occupation or field of work. We want to help them develop all the deep religious values that bring joy and satisfaction in doing their work as a part of their response to God's call. This is the heart of the task to which you have been called as a local church leader.[16]

Adult experience of the meaning of life, interpreted from the faith-perspective, is basic to giving the help youth have specifically requested. Teaching *about* life-choices, even by capable adults, cannot compensate for empty living in the world of Christian adults. But, as suggested in *You and Your Lifework,* when meaning *is* present, and when guidance is available, the experience of mature adults may be significant help.

Sex Education

Why does the subject of boy-girl relationships rank so high in the areas in which youth want help from the church? What can the church say or do that is distinct from what school and society do?

These questions are more easily asked than answered. Perhaps the heaping of attention upon sex, in reference to everything from band-aids to bathing suits, has the undesirable effect of producing an increasingly erotic society. Youth do not want to be left out of the "exciting" things that society has led them to anticipate in their relationship to members of the opposite sex. But movies and books and all manner of media provide adequate aid for meeting such interests. Youth must be seeking something else from the church. Conceivably, in the new openness about sex, they catch hints here and there about possibilities of meaning which the church can help them to understand. Such possibilities occasionally break through in the mass media—but they are also experienced personally as a boy and girl for the first time, in a glance, a touch, a moment of awareness, sense with wonder a whole new world opening before them. Perhaps youth want to know how to walk into the new world, to participate fully in it, and are asking help from the church in their search.

The church may be readier to give help now than it has ever been before. There seems to be a new willingness to affirm sexuality as a good and creative force, to explore ways in which that force can enable Christians—just because they *are* Christians—to perceive and experience deeper meaning in the totality of life. If the church is to meet the expressed concerns of youth, we will, with steady purpose, explore ways to interpret sexuality, to combine freedom with restraint, pleasure with responsibility, self-fulfillment with awareness of the other person.

At least three things can be said about the nature of the church's responsibility.

1. The whole scope of biblical and theological studies forms the solid foundation upon which any adequate sex education rests. Nevertheless, we must do more than we have in the past to give deliberate attention, where it is appropriate, to the meaning of sex within the basic studies themselves. In fact, the preaching, the youth-adult or congregational activities, all the life of the church, will provide opportunities to include sex education in natural, indirect ways.

2. The home occupies a key role in sex education. What children and youth see in their parents becomes educative. Therefore, adults need help in thinking through their own understanding of sex. They need to know how to live out that understanding, as well as to engage in conversations with their sons and daughters as there

is opportunity. Often, of course, youth may seem to hear other adults more readily, where sex is the subject, but even the casual comments or attitudes of parents are of major importance.

3. Specialized, short-term studies or retreats are among the most helpful, as well as the most popular ways in which the church may carry out its responsibilities for sex education. Here the more general considerations in basic studies of the Christian faith can be focused upon specific consideration of sex. Almost every denomination now offers help, in bibliographies, study unit outlines, audio-visual resource listings. The availability of such resources is mentioned here in order to encourage their use, though always under competent leadership.

Other ways of fulfilling responsibility will occur to the thoughtful adult who understands the pressures bearing upon youth in these days—youth who are asking for help from the church in achieving clarity in the midst of prevalent confusion. We can be too permissive or too legalistic, but neither extreme will meet the need of youth today. Only the Christian view of sexuality, with all its power and mystery, can meet that need.

A Comment

Again—a feeling of uneasiness. All of these programs and suggestions, and fifty others that could be named and described, may amount to exactly nothing. They may in effect be hindrances.

Or again, we wonder what can be accomplished. We are faced with the magnitude of our task, because from whatever angle we begin, we move inevitably to recognize that the equipping or nurturing process cannot be dealt with in piecemeal fashion. Nor can it be separated from vital participation in the ministry of the whole Christian community.

Looking realistically at the situation in the world, we Christians have to admit that conditions exist which all but deny the possibility of a Christian style of life for the young, growing laity, or for adults. But again we remind ourselves that we cannot wait to begin until we develop a perfect world or church or plan; our experience of dependence on God, as we recognize our inadequacies, may fashion us into more suitable instruments for his service.

IV

A Perspective:
Receiving and Responding
to the Gospel

Reconciliation to God is reconciliation to life itself . . .

—H. RICHARD NIEBUHR[1]

Since then I have given up the "religious" which is nothing but the exception, extraction, exaltation, ecstasy; or it has given me up. I possess nothing but the everyday out of which I am never taken. The mystery is no longer disclosed, it has escaped or it has made its dwelling here where everything happens as it happens. I know no fulness but each mortal hour's fulness of claim and responsibility. Though far from being equal to it, yet I know that in the claim I am claimed and may respond in responsibility, and know who speaks and demands a response.

—MARTIN BUBER[2]

11
Structure and Process
in Youth Ministry

"Heretical structures are structures which prevent the Gospel from reaching its intended goal."[1] This is the conclusion of one of the working groups in the World Council of Churches study on "The Missionary Structure of the Congregation." The World Council statement says, in effect, that forms, patterns—including organization and activities or processes that are emphasized or neglected or excluded—may be either a way of achieving a goal or an insurmountable barrier. Theologian Robert Clyde Johnson, including organization as a part of the whole area of church polity, speaks of a ministry of order. "On every level, and at every stage, order has a single purpose: *to enable the Church to deploy its forces most effectively in its assigned mission in and for the world.*"[2]

Dealing with so-called practical questions of the church's youth ministry takes on depth and importance when each concern is viewed as directly related to mission. Many such questions have already been raised; some are selected here for additional or more direct consideration. Each church, whether concerned with these areas or with others, will have to come to its own conclusions about how it organizes for work and how it carries out its agreed-upon tasks. These matters of organization and ways of going about our work are what we mean by structures.

Youth Structures

Are our structures good or bad, sound or "heretical"? Several questions may serve as guidelines for setting up structures or evaluating the existing structures.

1. Does the structure make it possible for youth to become involved in areas of ministry close at hand and throughout the world?

Sometimes ongoing church-wide structures—committees on witness or social action, for example—are cumbersome, but at least they point to ongoing areas of need, and they open doors for youth involvement. The first two cases studied in chapter 9 make that clear. In these cases provision was also made for immediate response to need wherever it might arise, with task force groups.

We recognize two problems, however. Critics convinced that the church is introverted and ineffective are calling for changes far more radical than shuffling or renaming committees. They are talking about setting up ministries nearer the point of need in the world, such as the school year ministry groups. Although youth structures may do some pioneering in this direction and thus contribute to the church as a whole, the likelihood is that they will operate *within* the framework set up by the church. Again, therefore, the suggestion is that what is happening in the church at large is more important than what is happening in youth work per se.

A second problem stems from the fact that, while structures can impede progress, they cannot guarantee attainment of goals. The attitudes and efforts of people bring life or death to that for which the structures exist. We hear the call to renewal in the very life of the church, not just in the forms through which life expresses itself. But here we have moved full circle—back to the point of our original consideration of mission. *If* there is a clear sense of mission, appropriate structures will emerge with the aid of free, responsible, *thinking* churchmen.

2. Does the structure make it possible to minister *to* youth, nurturing him within a fellowship where his personal needs are recognized and where he is sustained in his own ministering to others?

One of the conclusions reached in the Lutheran youth research, reported in *Profiles of Church Youth,* is this: "The pattern of most congregational programs militates against a personal approach to youth."[3] Because the realm of feelings and emotions looms so large for youth, as the documentation of this study makes clear, the conclusion is a discouraging one. In part, the problem is this:

Most pastors and lay leaders feel less competent to help in this area and as a result give little help. What they emphasize is precisely what they feel most competent to do—give information and exhort. A new awareness is needed of the total person and with it a conscious effort to bring the Word in a way that is meaningful and relevant to youth.[4]

In part, the trouble is in the adult's misconception of what troubles youth.

Accentuating the natural barrier of social distance between youth and adults is an unrealistic image which adults hold of youth. This image exaggerates their distress over family and dating problems and minimizes their concern over faith and unresolved guilt. It emphasizes their involvement in questionable activities and deemphasizes their sense of Christian vocation. Youth sense this caricature and feel unjustly judged. All of which reinforces their conviction that they are second-class citizens within the congregation. For this reason adults need to involve the youth in describing their needs and in helping to develop a youth program.[5]

Yet structures for ministry and structures for personal growth must not be set over against each other. As a person is caught up in mission, his commitment to that mission leads to personal freedom; his predicament is answered by God's love. The conscious support and awareness of the Christian community will help. If, within the existing structures—the action or ministry groups, the study groups, the church committees—an attempt is made to engage in a mutual ministry of personal concern and in a fellowship of prayer and study, surely the problem of need for support will be partly alleviated. And sometimes "the Great Conversation" or "the redemptive group" of which Ross Snyder speaks, dealing directly with the realm of feelings and emotions, will be for the world of adolescents the structure most directly contributory to mission.

Another aspect of the question about the relation of structures to personal need is the problem of ministering to the six-year range of youth from seventh through twelfth grades. Just as there is value in structures that relate youth to adults and encourage adult attitudes of respect and acceptance, so there is value in structures that provide relationships across the wide span of youth as well as those within a more limited age group. If graded study groups or classes can be coordinated through a council or central committee, it may be possible to conserve both values. A twelfth grader, for example, may learn a great deal in answering a seventh grader's question. If the scope of this book were limitless, a similar case could be made for structures which would relate youth to the children of the congregation in ways which would benefit *both* youth and children. In any event, the attitude of sensitivity to individuals within the structures is the chief essential in meeting personal needs.

3. Is the structure so designed as to unify the congregation across age-group lines, and at the same time to allow for particular contributions of various age groups and individuals?

Although priority is assigned to building youth integrally into the worship and work of the church, this emphasis should not be understood as absorbing youth, or molding them to conformity with established adult norms, or viewing them as adults. As in the illustrative cases in chapter 9, structures must open the way for youth to have a significant relationship to the congregation *and* to fellow youth.

> The young person moving toward adulthood needs both the verbal witness of Christian adults about the meaning of the Christian faith and their nonverbal acceptance and support. The willingness of adults to work and worship and study with him, recognizing him as a responsible participant in the witnessing Christian community, can mean as much to him as any statements he hears. This calls for a new recognition of the role adults can play in the Christian education of youth in which they should manifest grace in the face of his immaturity and uncertainty. But at the same time the church must continue to recognize the tremendous influence of the peer group, a group which is itself a potential channel for Christian communication. The young person requires the support of his peer group as he seeks his place in his own generation, but at the same time he must be protected from total reliance upon the immaturity and inexperience of himself and these same peers.[6]

Activities which are planned with peer groups should allow for both progression and diversity in program. In one church, adult leaders and seniors worked out an informal Sunday morning coffee hour for discussing paperback books, with youth serving as discussion leaders, and a plan for retreats to engage in basic biblical study. When eighth grade leaders decided to follow the same pattern (with cokes), the plan was spoiled for both age groups—in one case it was inappropriate; in the other, the uniqueness was destroyed by imitation. Seventh and eighth graders might do well to have a Friday afternoon and evening or a Saturday morning of study-activity time at the church, and defer Sunday night activities until they are older. Different emphases in camping programs, or work groups, or beyond-the-local-church activities would prevent repeating a particular pattern until it becomes "old stuff." Of course such planning cannot be effective apart from church-wide planning and recognition of ecumenical opportunities. It is essential also that youth themselves be involved in planning for particular situations. Effective structures will provide for coordination across and within age-group lines.

4. Are all structures clearly related to church government and discipline?

It is obvious that a pattern by which program is clearly related to denominational polity has both teaching value and efficiency. When the church's form of government has built-in provisions for ecumenical relationships, the particular structure is related immediately to the worldwide church.

5. Do the structures provide for experiences in the broader Christian fellowship, beyond the congregation?

The particular church is the matrix within which basic nurture takes place. That is the place of gathering and return after scattering; it is the place of continuing relationships. But it is important to provide exposure to the broader denominational fellowship as well as to the church universal. Perhaps the structures which point toward mission (as school year ministry groups) will serve the purpose. Rigid structures of a continuing, formal youth movement could defeat the purpose, as they sometimes have in the past. Short-term community, wider denominational, or ecumenical activities seem more appropriate for a vital engagement beyond the local church.

6. Do the structures at the same time provide for maintenance of continuing programs and relationships, but also allow for innovation?

If a study group or a task group wants to communicate with one of the church committees, is there a channel? Suppose a new idea occurs, a new opportunity develops, can that idea be handled or the opportunity be met quickly? In such situations there is need for some combination of continuity and flexibility like those described in chapter 9. There should be direct channels to the governing body of the church. The task force idea is widely in use as a means of investigating and undertaking specific tasks; when the assignment is completed, the task force is dissolved. We find increasingly an emphasis on swift change in strategy, on refusal to maintain forms that have outlived their usefulness. For a structure to have built into it the possibility of change or adaptation is a mark of wise planning and is the approach most appropriate for these shifting times.

Other questions might be added, on such points as the necessity for adequate administrative procedures if structures are to function effectively. The questions listed here will call attention to some of the concerns which are of major importance today for youth ministry.

The Teaching-Learning Process in Christian Education

What takes place when structure, purpose, activities, materials, become means by which people are nurtured in the faith? What kind of process is necessary if people are to be equipped for mission?

The second question was asked several years ago, as representatives from a group of denominations were developing plans for a new curriculum, to be known as the Covenant Life Curriculum. A basic paper was prepared which was later called "The Teaching-Learning Process to Be Used in the Educational Work of the Church." The title is unfortunate. "To be used" may suggest the existence of some specific procedure which can be utilized to "educate," and the term "teaching-learning" may suggest a formal classroom situation, an adult teacher-activity approach. Both assumptions are false. The statement is a description of what we may observe taking place as people receive and respond to the gospel. It is descriptive, not prescriptive. As described, the teaching-learning process deals with both questions raised in the preceding paragraph. It includes both study and ministry. It has to do with the interdependence of personal growth and discipleship. Excerpts from the description of each of the four aspects of the process describe something of its comprehensiveness.

Hearing or Listening

. . . The word "hearing" is crucial for Christian education, because it implies a word which when heard is dynamic and life-changing . . . . it suggests that one is taken hold of by something outside one's self, rather than that one merely learns about something which may or may not make a difference in one's life. The word "listening" is also crucial for the learning process, because it implies a willingness to hear, a voluntary activity in response to that which comes, a deliberate sensitiveness to the message that is contained in the words that fall on the ear or in the event which occurs.

Participation or Voluntary Involvement

Participation calls for an entering into or an identification with the story of God's redemption of mankind . . . .

Participation forbids the teacher or the learner to remain a spectator of God's work of redemption, requiring complete involvement with those to whom God comes, whether they be members of the historic community of the Old Testament or of the local congregation in which the teaching and learning are taking place . . . .

Exploration or Analysis

Exploration means applying one's mind critically to the Christian faith and to his own religious experience, thus helping one to grow in his own faith. It suggests the necessity to seek the demands of the Christian faith in all possible ways—analyzing the nature of the Bible and its manner of speaking, making full use of the principles of biblical interpretation in seeking its message, examining the nature and mission of the church and its relation to contemporary society, taking account of the possibilities and limitations of church programs and structures, making a critical appraisal of the situation in the world in which the church is placed . . . .

Accepting Responsibility or Undertaking

The fourth aspect of the learning process is accepting responsibility, both individually and corporately, or undertaking to carry out one's response to God in office, classroom, factory, wherever the Christian is found . . . . It makes plain the fact that the study program of the church must grow out of and lead into the church's total life of worship and work, and that study which is not related to the church's mission in the world is likely to be hollow mockery.[7]

A person "enters" the process anywhere, but the movement from that point must lead to all other aspects, not necessarily in any certain order, or in any certain schedule, or to any certain place. Sometimes they happen simultaneously. There are many "teachers"—parents, preachers, adult leaders, laymen in the world who share in the "analysis" of the gospel's presence in their midst. The kind of learning of which we are speaking is not confined to the classroom. It may seem to occur there, but it may seem to occur also in the "world" in the moment of undertaking an act of obedience. When it really does happen, this learning which is a change in the self and a deeper faithfulness to mission, it pulls together all the phases of the process, perhaps in a moment of insight or mental structuring of relationships. Whether one is describing the teaching-learning process or involvement in mission, the process is the same—that by which *the world* receives and responds to the gospel.

The Church's Youth Ministry

Looking back at the book as a whole from the perspective now gained, we can see a frame of reference, or better, a unifying process (which we have called teaching-learning) by which we can understand the relationship between some of the areas we have explored—between belief and behavior, ministry and nurture, reflection and action. We see that youth cannot be educated now in anticipation of undertaking responsibility later. The undertaking is a continuing part of the process which makes education possible. Or again, youth cannot be isolated. They must identify with, participate in, the total life of the church. As the whole church must reflect upon its heritage, its purpose, its present situation, so youth voluntarily involve themselves in the reflecting and the shaping of decisions. Youth do not have to duplicate in their peer group activities the experiences which occur elsewhere in the congregation. Each group in the church need not try to do or to be everything, because its particular function is always to be viewed as a part of the whole process. The life of the smaller group exists within the life of the body, and its health derives from the health of the body.

If the process is to be dynamic, not static, we cannot work with a rigid structure or a circumscribed program. But we can provide some beginnings we know are needed—in worship, in study, in planning and engaging in the work of the church, perhaps with variation in schedule and setting. We can begin to include youth as young laity in the life and work of the church. And if we care enough about the mission assigned to us, the next steps will come clear.

> But never does youth offer as faithful a picture of its true spirit or show its virtues so strikingly or its faults so glaringly, never are the talents of youth so richly exploited or youth's love of risk put to greater test than when the world itself is in a state of rejuvenation as it obviously is today.[8]

It is in such a time that we are fashioning a youth ministry. *Can* we bring the Christian dimension into youth's talents and love of risk so that they, and we all, the people of God, become involved in this rejuvenescence of the world?

12
The Adult as Servant-Leader

What adults are called into the church's ministry with youth? Anyone may be. There is no check list of qualities, age, desired appearance. Adults are needed who are not afraid to take initiative as leaders, but who know themselves to be servants. Those are needed who are willing to pay the cost in terms of time, entering uncertain territory and digging deep to find their way, and perhaps most of all in terms of caring—for the young people individually, about the church's faithfulness generally. And those are needed who can receive into themselves with gratitude the blessings that result from paying that cost.

Some of the functions most frequently required of adult leaders are reviewed in this chapter, as are questions about authority and the role of the adult. What is said may help a worker to review his responsibility or to anticipate something of what is involved in it.

Teaching

What is it to teach? One teacher of youth, commenting on her first teaching opportunity, said, "I have been confronted by an urgent demand *to know for myself*. Something keeps coming through to me and pushing me to find out, not just in order to teach, but because the subject is important." Her students—though she did not know it—commented on her ability to make things clear, her willingness to think with them in her questions and in her expression of convictions. Evidently ideas were offered openly, not dogmatically, for consideration by the group.

One of the first things teaching means is having something to start with in terms of knowledge about the designated subject. Students in both public schools and church schools are constant in their appreciation for people who have competence in the field in which they teach. Neither warmth in relationships nor sparkling personality can compensate for a vacuum in knowledge.

Not that the teacher has to know everything. That would be impossible anyway, but defeating if it were possible. Students appreciate teachers who keep on learning and are excited about doing it. Not that teachers have to verbalize their knowledge or express their convictions as habitual procedure. There must be a rightness of time and occasion for such an offering. One teen-ager spoke in class one Sunday. "Miss Smith, what does Jesus Christ mean to you?" Fellow classmates immediately chimed in with answers. The boy interrupted. "You guys shut up. I want to know what Miss Smith thinks." Miss Smith tried to say. To have made such a speech without the query or to have offered a testimony each week would have been an imposition. Here, it was a serious answer to a serious question. Teaching has to do with a willingness to offer one's knowledge for the benefit of the group, even with the awareness of one's own limited understanding.

A second thing teaching means is that the teacher is able to structure situations in which people learn. The implications of that simple statement are amazing. Learning situations have to do with the whole process of receiving the gospel, and may include all informal conversations and planned ministries; but here they will refer especially to those planned occasions in which study is the central activity. The important thing is to involve the learner in responsibility for his own learning. Nobody else can learn for him. Telling him he is responsible does no good, of course. Some other things may: causing him to *think,* through the use of questions; involving him in investigation and reports where class periods are long enough; encouraging his theologizing about the meaning of experience; motivating outside study. *Telling* him he should do outside study is not motivating it. Nebulous assignments ("study the lesson for next time") and lectures for failure to study those nebulous assignments are inexcusable. The making of individual, specific, varied assignments, with adult help provided where it is needed, is the kind of structuring that a skilled teacher will do for activities during as well as outside the class.

Teaching means other things, too—more than can be enumerated here. A comment about team teaching, however, is in order. Where people can complement each other in their abilities and knowledge, and support each other in their efforts, a more effective job is often the result. Team teaching means planning everything together, from purpose to the procedure of every session, and designating individual responsibility. Sometimes one person does all the teaching; sometimes there is dialogue; sometimes there is work with the total group, one leading a discussion, another telling a story; sometimes there is group work. Obviously, just taking turns teaching, by week or month, is not team teaching. Real team teaching probably requires more work than teaching alone. However, students see people thinking and working together. They benefit from the broadened scope of experience and knowledge brought by the teachers to the situation. Variations of the teaching team idea are being experimented with. All of them, and new ones to be devised, are possibilities for the church.

Planning

Adults plan with youth in many ways. Planning will become an even more important skill of the adult leader than it now is if the work of church committees, mission-oriented groups involved in investigation into both heritage and world, and task force groups achieve the place of importance they have been assigned.

The rather specific procedure suggested for planning in service and witness on page 107 is adaptable for any task-oriented group. The movement is something like this:

Clarification of task
Securing needed information
Devising a procedure for action
Assigning responsibility

That general sequence, with variations, may help to give a committee or council an idea about steps in planning. The adult works with youth in planning for the planning (and uses the recommended procedure in doing so); he helps in the process with questions and comments, where necessary; he follows through on the plans made.

In preparation for teaching, a somewhat different approach to planning may be desirable. Very often teachers or program advisers have interpreted planning as being directed to *how* we shall conduct the class or present the program. Sometimes, of course, that is exactly what is expected; in that case, the approach to planning summarized in the preceding paragraph is applicable. On the other hand, if planning can be directed more to consideration of content or subject matter, a more profitable use of students' limited time can be the result. Furthermore, the teacher may receive more help in discovering what questions and concerns face young people in a particular subject. Here are two illustrations, with different approaches suggested by differing instructions given by the teacher.

1. "Let's take the first thirty minutes and read chapter 3. Mark the sections you feel you've already covered with an X. Check sections with a V that you feel would be most valuable to you right now. Write out specific additional questions as they occur, in the margin of the text."

Here the whole group is involved in planning. Either the teacher or a small committee of two or three could work through the results of the chapter previewed. What happens is that the group is drawn into the subject and motivated to pursue certain lines of investigation. A planning committee, or whoever does the job of determining how to follow up on expressed interests, may use the general planning pattern suggested for a task group.

There is rarely any good purpose to be served by approaches like these: "What do you want to study in the next chapter?" (Nothing!) "What questions do you have about _____?" (None!) Getting *into* the subject in some way is ordinarily a better procedure than "What do you want to do?"

2. "The three teams into which we've just divided will have one chapter each to work on for class today, and then, as needed, to work on later. Your assignment is to read through your chapter individually, then as a group to make a list of topics or questions you think we should consider in our study of _____ . You will then be responsible for working with me [or us, in team teaching] in teaching that chapter. I have done some preliminary work with your chairman, and he will know how to pick up at that point."

Notice that the "how" is considered here, but only after the "what"; method is dealt with only because youth making decisions will have responsibility for carrying out their plans—and learning from evaluating them.

In the first illustration, the emphasis is on total group planning, with the possibility that a planning committee may follow through. In the second illustration, planning began when the teacher met with those who would be chairmen of work groups. Each work group then operated as a planning committee. Besides these two ways, there are others in which planning committees may function. Sometimes a specially appointed or elected committee can work outside class with the teacher for planning a unit of work. Sometimes group teams are set up and rotate planning responsibilities.

Planning itself is teaching. Or learning. And the principle of adults planning with youth is more important by far than the use of a plan that worked for someone else. In fact, it may be better to vary the planning procedures, and to use procedures that make sense to the teacher at a given time for a given class and a given subject matter.

Evaluating

Evaluating, like planning, is an essential activity in the process we have been considering, that of relating church to world to personal faith. It becomes a means of learning from what has happened, as well as a way to improve future enterprises.

Technically, evaluation has to do with measuring outcomes or results against clearly stated, specific purposes. We need help from professionals in the field of research in just this fashion at many points in our youth ministry.

Then there is the kind of evaluating which always goes on in tests, answers to questions, reports, informal evaluation in comments, reaction (or feedback) to what is going on.

There are other ways in which evaluation can be planned as an integral part of learning and of service. The questions on page 101 are suggestive of an approach to a service project or task group's work. As a part of study, and as an aid to learning, evaluation may be approached like this:

What did we learn during our study of _____? or, What is the
   most important thing you have learned during our study of
   _____ ? or, What was the most significant thing that happened to you during our study of _____?
What areas did we neglect that you were interested in?
Could we have carried out our study in a way that would have
   been more helpful and more interesting? How?
Have we helped each other in our learning? or, Have we been
   responsible members of this group? or, Have we been aware
   of one another as persons?

Questionnaires, papers, almost any teaching technique can be
used in evaluation. The *way* evaluation is carried out teaches something. Some inquiries teach students to sit back as spectators and
judge the performance of others, their teachers or their peers: "Did
you like this study? this program? How can I make it more interesting for you?" There may be situations when that kind of question
has validity, but not many.

Then there is the personal evaluation by an adult leader for
himself, or by a group of adult leaders working together. When we
learn to evaluate ourselves, honestly and objectively, and when we
learn how to learn from our failures, youth will benefit.

Being Available

Though we sometimes speak of counseling, that is too technical
a term for what most of us do as adult leaders. Neither are the terms
guiding or interviewing—suggested as less technical substitutes for
counseling—entirely satisfactory. Whatever the function is labeled,
adults are often consulted or called upon in times of problems
or decisions. Most of us know some of the simple guidelines for
our response, as we try to accept the teen-ager and help set him
free from his frustrations and fears. Sometimes listening is all that
is needed—*really* listening, however, with one's whole self. A young
person may feel that no one is particularly interested in him;
when he finds a sympathetic person, he feels understood. Arguing,
judging, making a person's decision for him—these are of no help.
If we are trying to understand the person, we will move so closely

with him and his account that we could not judge if we would. But in the moving closely with him, we must be objective; we must not excuse any more than condemn. Our task is to see clearly, to help a person isolate his problem, analyze it, formulate and work toward solutions. Being willing to give help means learning to keep confidences, and learning to release people from dependence on us. Sometimes adult leaders unintentionally build dependence, thus "using" young people to satisfy their own needs. A brief reflection on such aspects of another "difficult business of helping" may suggest to us the desirability of increasing our competence in this area.

But no matter how skilled or knowledgeable we are, if we ourselves are not really available, our ministry is negligible. Speaking of troubled adolescents, professionals say that "knowledge without *feeling* may be useless."[1] Martin Buber, one of the great Jewish teacher-theologians of this century, in reporting a conversation with a student, says this:

> I conversed attentively and openly with him—only I omitted to guess the questions which he did not put. Later, not long after, I learned from one of his friends—he himself was no longer alive— the essential content of these questions; I learned that he had come to me not casually, but borne by destiny, not for a chat but for a decision. He had come to me, he had come in this hour. What do we expect when we are in despair and yet go to a man? Surely a presence by means of which we are told that nevertheless there is meaning.[2]

Perhaps all the possible functions of the adult leader come together in that phrase—"a presence by means of which we are told that nevertheless there is meaning."

The Question of Authority

In response to what is generally regarded as youth's lack of respect for authority in our time, someone may be saying, How can we acquire the authority we need to do all these things? It is true that the whole area of authority is awry these days. Traditional authority—established norms of conduct or belief, or of age or office in persons—seems as unimpressive to adults as to youth.

One teen-ager on our youth panel said, in speaking of adult-youth relationships, "It seems to me adults are afraid of us. They know how much we learn in school these days, and they don't trust themselves." The discussion that followed pointed up the fact that youth look for integrity, concern, and evidence of openness to new knowledge as crucial factors in calling forth respect and response.

Indeed, there is evidence to suggest that ours is a time when authority is either intrinsic or practically nonexistent, when it must be earned, not demanded. Youth respond to inner authority, as adults do. They *say* they do, and evidence substantiates their claim. Adults may find this a rather threatening statement, because it challenges us to do an effective job.

Even parents cannot rely on the assumption that they have authority which their sons and daughters will accept. Sometimes parents are inconsistent about expectations and rules: "Other parents do it," they say, or they take the easy way of being arbitrarily rigid or lazily permissive. Authority vanishes as parental unpredictability increases. There *are* cultural factors, however, that are difficult to overcome—indeed, impossible to overcome without changes more drastic than we can effect. All adult leaders, including parents, need to look seriously at the necessity for a secure framework within which children and youth can find freedom. As we try to help provide that framework, with steadiness, consistency, and self-discipline about growing into the responsibility we have accepted, the authority we need may be granted to us.

How Shall We Present Ourselves?

An adult leader at one of the consultations on youth ministry raised the question, "How shall we present ourselves?" The question is a good one. What, in the back of his mind, is the self-image of who he is and what he is for, that guides an adult worker in offering himself and his services to youth?

Terms like leader, teacher, adviser, guide, counselor are used. Some people prefer a term like enabler to suggest what the adult worker's essential function is in relation to youth. Albert H. van den Heuvel, recognizing the influence adults in general have on youth, raises the question as to what the "new adult" is like.

> Little has been done about describing the new adult. He will
> be the man whom Kierkegaard tried to paint in his essay on the
> Knight of Faith (although few living people will ever arrive at
> such emotional stability); he will be the man whom Bonhoeffer
> called the man come of age.[3]

This image that Van den Heuvel holds before both youth and adults
has characteristics of flexibility, trustworthiness, curiosity, an experimental attitude, a willingness to meditate and to listen. Many of
these are the same qualities as those adolescents are being forced to
develop in a rapidly changing society.

In his book *Young Man Luther,* Erik Erikson speaks of the
need youth have for adults who will be "guarantors of their established identity."[4] This adult is himself a mature person who can offer the younger person a combination of acceptance and firmness.
Ross Snyder sees the adult guarantor as personifying the role which
can best serve youth in our society.

> This discovery of the adult guarantor, we believe, opens a
> new, yet old, relationship in the church's work with youth. It pro-
> vides a model for the adult counselor with any young group and
> for other adult members of the church who are related to young
> people.[5]

The following quotation is an excerpt from a fuller description
of the guarantor role.

> A guarantor is a significant other, who is farther along in
> life, who establishes us with a co-personal world. Knowing that
> he cannot live our life for us, but only affirm us as true and give
> us entree. "Entree" means both "the main course of the feast of
> life," and "the right and freedom to enter."
>
> A guarantor is not a father-mother substitute, but an adult
> who has a respected place in some activity valued by us, who
> notices us personally, talks to us as an equal, and by his depend-

able image of us enables us to feel 'being the kind of person I am, I will make it.' He is experienced primarily as one who enjoys me, thinks I am worthy of being listened to and understood. A person I click with.

Whatever our age, we need a guarantor as we work into the inner circle of some new-for-us enterprise, having to become a new person in the process.

We need such a person as a *reference point of identity* within ourselves. Also as a source of courage. For we can stand up to change and tension, grow by leaps and risk, only if something remains throughout it all, i.e., relationship with a guarantor. A person who trusts us and we trust, *continues* us.

A guarantor firms in us expectation—as contrasted with wispy dreaming which we know is largely illusion. We begin, not only to vision the good life, to feel vaguely that we are desirable life, but to feel that it will come off. (Expectation is always both a *vision* of the desirable and a *belief that it will happen*.) Being what we are, we have a real chance in life. We can count on being something special.

Introduced by the guarantor, we become—often to our surprise—weavers of the social fabric. He does this partly by clueing others on the expectation they may have of us. Somewhat as when a person takes us to a social event and introduces us around, at first we are accepted not because of what we are (for no one knows that yet), but because someone has, in effect, said to both the introduced people, "You two are not enemies; neither of you are carrying concealed weapons, you can be trusted, something interesting may happen."[6]

How shall we present ourselves? Whatever our answer, our hope is clear—that our ministry will be used by God to bring to young laity something of his power and glory, and a sense of responsible freedom that sends them on mission into his world.

The People of God

More important than a list of responsibilities of an adult leader is his view of himself and his role, his guiding image—as that of guarantor—which may serve as a reference point for specific decisions, attitudes, acts. More important than his individual work or his role is the existence and the mission of the whole people of God, to which both he and young laity belong.

What is the significance of attaching such importance to "the existence and the mission of the whole people of God"? Several things are implied:

> That we adults responsible for the church's ministry with youth do not work alone. God himself is active through his people in the world he has created. The communion of saints, past, present, and future, sustains us.

> That we can work with the hope and expectation that our momentary failures can be overcome, that our human efforts, our imperfect but reformable structures, do not limit God and the ultimate working out of his purpose for mankind.

> That our call is to enter with young laity into God's mission in his world. We are not dealing with trivial matters. It is God's purpose that persons should be transformed into new creations, and as his disciples, enter into the ministry of reconciliation. This is the context for the church's ministry with youth. What we do in worship, conversations, study groups, ministry groups, can be understood properly only when placed in this context.

We gain a perspective from approaching our work in this way. Somehow we are made confident that the church will open itself to renewal, that reconciliation between generations can occur within the Christian community, that God's people will engage in ministry wherever thay are stationed in the world. Our participation in ministry is our response to the gospel we have received—and in the responding we receive ever more fully the meaning and the power of that gospel.

Acknowledgments

PART I. THE MINISTRY OF RECONCILIATION

1. William Stringfellow, *A Private and Public Faith* (Grand Rapids: Wm. B. Eerdmans Publishing Co., 1962), p. 41. Used by permission.

2. *Ibid.*, p. 63.

Chapter 1. "Thanks Be to God"

1. Dian Molton, "The BYF: An Elephant Story," *The High Call* (American Baptist), Vol. 16, No. 2 (Spring, 1965), p. 9.

2. Christopher S. Dann and Charles R. McManis, Youth Associates. Reported by Virginia M. Harbour, "A Platform for Youth Work." From the *International Journal of Religious Education*, Vol. 40, No. 7 (March, 1964), p. 8. Copyright, Division of Christian Education, National Council of Churches. Used by permission.

3. Wallace McPherson Alston, *A History of Young People's Work in the Presbyterian Church in the United States (1861–1938)* (Doctoral thesis, Union Theological Seminary, Richmond, Virginia, 1943), p. 90.

4. *Ibid.*, p. 128.

5. *Ibid.*, p. 291.

6. *We Have This Ministry . . . 1. The Objective of Christian Education for Senior High Young People* (New York: Division of Christian Education, Department of Youth Work, National Council of Churches, 1958), pp. 14–15.

Chapter 2. "God So Loved the World . . ."

1. Walter M. Abbott, S.J. (ed.), *The Documents of Vatican II* (New York: The America Press, 1966), p. 235.

2. "The Directory for the Worship and Work of the Church," in *The Book of Church Order of the Presbyterian Church in the United States* (rev. ed., 1963), §§ 223–1, 2, 3.

3. *Principles of Church Union* (Cincinnati: Forward Movement Publications, 1966), p. 14. By permission.

4. *Ibid.*, pp. 26–27.

5. William A. Yon, "Youth on Mission," *Student World* (Geneva: World Student Christian Federation), Vol. LVI, No. 4, 1963, p. 307.

6. Abbott, *op. cit.*, p. 350.

7. From *The Humiliation of the Church*, by Albert H. van den Heuvel, p. 106. The Westminster Press. Copyright © 1966, W. L. Jenkins. Used by permission. Also by permission of SCM Press Ltd., London.

8. *Ibid.*, p. 109.

9. *Ibid.*

10. *Ibid.*, pp. 109–110.

Chapter 3. "God's Own People"

1. Robert Clyde Johnson (ed.), *The Church and Its Changing Ministry* (Philadelphia: Office of the General Assembly, The United Presbyterian Church U.S.A., 1961), p. 26.

2. *Ibid.*, p. 29.

3. Sara Little, *The Language of the Christian Community* (Richmond: The CLC Press, 1965), p. 5.

4. *Ibid.*

5. Quoted in Robert Simpson, "They Gave Up! I Quit!" *Youth* (United Church of Christ), Vol. 17, No. 6 (March 13, 1966), p. 18.

6. *Ibid.*, p. 19.

7. Quoted in Albert H. van den Heuvel (ed.), *The New Creation and the New Generation* (New York: Friendship Press, 1965), p. 55.

8. Albert H. van den Heuvel, "A Short and Critical History of Youth Work," in *ibid.*

9. *Ibid.*, p. 56.

10. Marshall McLuhan, *Understanding Media: The Extensions of Man* (New York: McGraw-Hill Book Co., 1964), p. 4.

11. *Ibid.*, p. 5.

12. *Ibid.*, p. 347.

13. Donald N. Michael, *The Next Generation* (New York: Random House, Inc., Vintage Book ed., 1963, 1965), p. 83.

14. *Ibid.*, p. 185.

15. *Ibid.*, p. 173.

16. René Maheu, "Youth with a Purpose," *The Unesco Courier* (July-August, 1965), p. 7.

17. Acher Deleon, "More Than 1,000 Million Under-25's," in *ibid.*, p. 51.

18. Grace and Fred M. Hechinger, "In the Time It Takes You to Read These Lines the American Teen-ager Will Have Spent $2,378.22," *Esquire*, Vol. LXIV, No. 1 (July, 1965), p. 65.

19. *Ibid.*

20. *Ibid.*

21. William Troy, "Dialogue Is a Song and Dance," *Focus* (United Church of Christ), Fall, 1966, p. 12.

22. *Ibid.*, p. 14.

23. *Ibid.*

24. Merton P. Strommen, *Profiles of Church Youth* (St. Louis: Concordia Publishing House, 1963), p. ix. By permission.

25. *Ibid.*, p. x.

26. From *Anne Frank: The Diary of a Young Girl*, p. 164.

27. Hechinger and Hechinger, *op. cit.*, p. 31.

28. Strommen, *op. cit.*, p. 107.

29. David Mallery, *High School Students Speak Out* (New York: Harper & Row, Publishers, Inc., 1962), p. 113.

30. *Ibid.*, p. 59.

31. Erik H. Erikson, "Youth and the Life Cycle," *Children*, Vol. 7, No. 2 (March-April, 1960), pp. 43–49. Erikson's theory is developed more fully in his book *Childhood and Society*.

32. Erik H. Erikson, *Young Man Luther* (New York: W. W. Norton & Co., Inc., 1958).

33. Erikson, in *Children, op. cit.,* p. 46.

34. *Ibid.*

35. William Ellery Leonard, "I Feel Me Near to Some High Thing," in *Voices of America,* eds. Leonidas Warren Payne, Jr., Mark A. Neville, Natalie E. Chapman (Chicago: Rand McNally & Co., 1941), p. 460. By permission.

36. *Anne Frank,* p. 13.

37. Lewis Joseph Sherrill, *The Struggle of the Soul* (New York: The Macmillan Co., 1951), p. 65.

PART II. INVOLVEMENT IN MISSION

Chapter 4. Illustrative Studies: Scenes of Ministry

1. *Scenes of Witness* (Lansing, Ill.: Reformed Church in America, Office of Evangelism, n.d.), p. 1.

2. "God Speaks Through the Prophets," *Studies in Christian Living* (The Methodist Church), Vol. 9, No. 3 (Summer, 1961), p. 3.

3. Quoted in Greg Hurlburt, "A High School Talks Back," *Hi Way* (The United Presbyterian Church U.S.A.).

4. Stringfellow, *A Private and Public Faith,* p. 54.

5. George F. MacLeod, *Only One Way Left* (Glasgow/Iona/Edinburgh: The Iona Community, 1956), pp. 141–142.

6. J. Edward Swain, "A Church Ministry *to, by,* and *with* Youth," *Focus* (Fall, 1964), p. 15.

7. *Ibid.*

8. *Ibid.*

9. Publicity brochure from Mecklenburg Presbytery, Presbyterian Church in the United States.

Chapter 5. Where Mission Takes Place

1. Don Knipschield, "Laborers of Love," *Classmate* (The Methodist Church), Vol. 73, No. 9 (May, 1966), p. 9.

2. William J. Fogleman, *I Live in the World* (Richmond: The CLC Press, 1966), p. 55.

3. Donald W. Shriver, Jr., *How Do You Do—And Why?* (Richmond: The CLC Press, 1966), p. 105.

4. *Ibid.,* pp. 112–113.

5. Roy W. Fairchild, *Christians in Families* (Richmond: The CLC Press, 1964), p. 226.

6. Grace Nies Fletcher, *What's Right with Our Young People* (New York: Whiteside, Inc., 1966), pp. 112–113.

7. Marguerite and Frank Fidler, *Can't Help Wondering* (New York: Friendship Press, 1967), p. 67.

8. Jared Rardin, "How Forms of Ministry Can Respond," *Dimensions of Ministry in an Urban Society,* Papers and Proceedings of the First General Committee, Department of Youth Ministry, National Council of Churches, 1965, p. 59.

9. *Ibid.,* p. 62.

10. *Ibid.,* p. 63.
11. *Ibid.,* p. 59.
12. *Ibid.,* p. 63.
13. *Ibid.,* pp. 59–60.
14. *Ibid.,* p. 63.
15. As reported by Miss Glenda Briscoe, Director of Christian Education.
16. "In the Fellowship of Errors," *The Presbyterian Outlook,* Vol. 148, No. 29 (August 8, 1966), p. 7.
17. "Ecumenical High School Encounters; Thrust III—School Year Ministry Groups," Section II, Projects, *Folio—1963* (New York: Department of Youth Work, National Council of Churches, and the United Christian Youth Movement, 1963), no page numbers.
18. *Ibid.*
19. L. E. McRobert, "Parkersburg's Hope Corps," *Workers with Youth* (The Methodist Church), Vol. 19, No. 10 (June, 1966), p. 16.
20. Mary E. and Dick Denman, "Project in Learning," *Classmate,* Vol. 73, No. 3 (November, 1965), pp. 17–19.
21. Sheila D. Woods, *Youth Ventures Toward a Vital Church* (New York: Abingdon Press, 1965), p. 205. By permission.
22. Douglas R. Trottier, "The Fish—A Coffeehouse for Youth," *Focus* (Winter, 1966), p. 16.
23. *Ibid.*
24. *Ibid.,* p. 15.
25. *Ibid.,* p. 16.
26. *Ibid.*
27. Letter to the author.
28. Albert H. van den Heuvel, "We Shall Know Only What We Do!" *Study Encounter* (Geneva: Division of Studies, World Council of Churches), Vol. I, No. 4, 1965, p. 189.
29. As reported by Miss Bettye Killgore, Director of Christian Education.
30. John Barbour, "Young Lives on the Line for Others," in the *Charlotte Observer,* June 12, 1966, p. 1A.
31. David Gottlieb and Charles E. Ramsey, *The American Adolescent* (Homewood, Ill.: The Dorsey Press, Inc., 1964), p. 69.
32. *Ibid.,* p. 70.
33. *Presence,* World Student Christian Federation, 1965–1968, p. 2.

Chapter 6. "This Difficult Business of Helping"

1. Alan Keith-Lucas, *This Difficult Business of Helping* (Richmond: The CLC Press, 1965), p. 4.
2. *Ibid.,* pp. 12–13.
3. John Calvin, *Institutes of the Christian Religion,* trans. Henry Beveridge (2 vols.; London: James Clarke & Co., 1949), Bk. III, Chap. VII, §§ 1–2.
4. Stringfellow, *A Private and Public Faith,* pp. 83–84.
5. Keith-Lucas, *op. cit.,* p. 27.
6. Harvey Cox, *The Secular City* (New York: The Macmillan Co.), pp. 139–140. Copyright © Harvey Cox 1965. By permission.
7. *Ibid.,* p. 141.
8. Gordon W. Allport, *The Individual and His Religion* (New York: The Macmillan Co., 1950), p. 64.

9. Mathews F. Allen, Jr., and Betsy Rice, *Youth in the Church's Mission, 1964–65* (Richmond: The CLC Press, 1964), p. 28.

10. *Ibid.*, p. 30, adapted.

PART III. EQUIPPING YOUNG LAITY

1. John A. Mackay, *God's Order* (New York: The Macmillan Co., 1953), p. 149.

Chapter 7. Education and Mission

1. Van den Heuvel, *The Humiliation of the Church*, p. 110.

2. H. Richard Niebuhr, *The Purpose of the Church and Its Ministry*, pp. 127 –128, copyright © 1956 Harper and Brothers reprinted with the permission of Harper & Row, Publishers, Inc., New York.

3. Maheu, in *The Unesco Courier, op. cit.*, p. 6.

4. James M. Gustafson, *Treasure in Earthen Vessels* (New York: Harper & Row, Publishers, Inc., 1961), p. 51.

5. *Ibid.*

6. Ross Snyder, "The Ministry of Meaning," *Risk* (Geneva: Youth Departments of the World Council of Churches and World Council of Christian Education), Vol. I, Nos. 3 and 4 (1965), pp. 131–135.

7. *Ibid.*, p. 135.

8. *Ibid.*, p. 134.

9. Rardin, in *Dimensions of Ministry in an Urban Society*, p. 67.

10. Veronique Laufer, "The Call to Service," in *ibid.*, p. 55.

11. *Ibid.*, p. 56.

Chapter 8. The School and General Education

1. From *Youth Kit*, No. 21, p. 12. The Geneva Press. Copyright © 1963, W. L. Jenkins. Used by permission.

2. *Ibid.*, p. 13.

3. *Ibid.*, p. 14.

4. *Ibid.*

5. *Ibid.*, p. 15.

6. Rardin, in *Dimensions of Ministry in an Urban Society*, pp. 65–66.

7. *Folio—1964* (New York: Department of Youth Work, National Council of Churches, and the United Christian Youth Movement, 1964), p. 97. This is a summary of procedures more fully described in *Folio—1963*.

8. Theodore McEachern, "Some Possible Models for Local Ecumenical Encounter," in *ibid.*, p. 96.

9. Frances Eastman, "Christian Faith and Public School Learnings: The Through-the-Week Series," *International Journal of Religious Education*, Vol. 42, No. 11 (July-August, 1966), pp. 14–16, 37.

10. Quoted from the Abington vs. Schempp decisions of the Supreme Court, June 17, 1963, in Rolfe Lanier Hunt, "These Things Public Schools May Do." From the *International Journal of Religious Education*, Vol. 42, No. 8 (April, 1966), p. 16. Copyright, Division of Christian Education, National Council of Churches. Used by permission.

11. *Ibid.*, p. 17.

12. *Ibid.*

Chapter 9. Illustrative Studies: Scenes of Nurture

1. *I Was a Teen-age Communicant* (Philadelphia: Board of Christian Education, The United Presbyterian Church U.S.A., n.d.), p. 4. The section summarized here covers pages 32–45.
2. *Ibid.*, pp. 36–39.
3. Idea based on plans worked out in Brazos Presbytery, Texas, under the leadership of Miss Florine Miller.
4. Betsy Rice, *Youth in the Church* (Richmond: The CLC Press, 1963), pp. 65–66.
5. Henry N. Tani, *Ventures in Youth Work* (Philadelphia: The Christian Education Press, 1957), p. 170.
6. Based on chapter 11 of *Ventures in Youth Work,* as developed in *Leading Young People* (Greenwich, Conn.: The Seabury Press, 1961), p. 29.
7. Snyder, *Risk, op. cit.,* pp. 7–9.
8. *Ibid.,* pp. 16–18.
9. *Ibid.,* pp. 59–60.

Chapter 10. Areas of Concern

1. *Principles of Church Union,* p. 30.
2. Erik Routley, *Hymns Today and Tomorrow* (New York: Abingdon Press, 1964), p. 18.
3. Snyder, *Risk, op. cit.,* pp. 65–66.
4. William Robert Miller, *The World of Pop Music and Jazz* (St. Louis: Concordia Publishing House, 1965), p. 96.
5. Snyder, *op. cit.,* pp. 68–69.
6. Strommen, *Profiles of Church Youth,* p. 105.
7. *Ibid.*
8. Shriver, *How Do You Do—And Why?,* p. 108.
9. "Youth and Adults Engage in Dialogue," *Our Job* (The United Presbyterian Church U.S.A.), Vol. 18, No. 4 (December, 1966), p. 2.
10. Shriver, *op. cit.,* pp. 118–119.
11. *The Book of Church Order,* § 210–1.
12. *Ibid.,* § 210–2.
13. J. Will Ormond, *Youth Entering Into Covenant: For Pastor and Session* (Richmond: The CLC Press, 1965), pp. 4–5.
14. *Ibid.,* p. 4.
15. Strommen, *op. cit.,* p. 189.
16. Albert Curry Winn, *Local Church Leader's Guide to You and Your Lifework: A Christian Choice for Youth* (Chicago: Science Research Associates, Inc., 1963), p. 3.

PART IV. A PERSPECTIVE:
RECEIVING AND RESPONDING TO THE GOSPEL

1. Niebuhr, *The Purpose of the Church and Its Ministry,* p. 37.
2. Martin Buber, *Between Man and Man,* trans. Ronald Gregor Smith (New York: The Macmillan Co.), p. 14. Copyright © 1965, The Macmillan Company. By permission. Also by permission of Routledge & Kegan Paul, Ltd., London.

Chapter 11. Structure and Process in Youth Ministry

1. Quoted in Colin W. Williams, *Where in the World?* (New York: National Council of Churches, 1963), p. 83.

2. Johnson, *The Church and Its Changing Ministry,* p. 21.

3. Strommen, *Profiles of Church Youth,* p. 238.

4. *Ibid.,* p. 239.

5. *Ibid.,* pp. 239–240.

6. *Principles for the Development of Curriculum for Youth,* Principles Paper V (Richmond: Board of Christian Education, Presbyterian Church, U.S., 1961), p. 5.

7. *The Teaching-Learning Process to Be Used in the Educational Work of the Church,* Foundation Paper V (Richmond: Board of Christian Education, Presbyterian Church, U.S.), pp. 6–7.

8. Maheu, in *The Unesco Courier, op. cit.,* p. 5.

Chapter 12. The Adult as Servant-Leader

1. J. Roswell Gallagher and Herbert I. Harris, *Emotional Problems of Adolescents* (New York: Oxford University Press, 1958), p. 4.

2. Buber, *Between Man and Man,* p. 14.

3. Van den Heuvel, in *The New Creation and the New Generation,* p. 70.

4. Erikson, *Young Man Luther,* p. 125.

5. Ross Snyder, "Christianity and Young People: An Interpretation from the Point of View of Theology and Existence," in *The New Creation and the New Generation,* p. 40.

6. Snyder, *Risk, op. cit.,* pp. 137–138.

Selected Index